WOMEN IN WORKFORCE - BALANCING IDENTITY & MARITAL BOND

THIS BOOK IS BASED ON DR REKHA RANI'S RESEARCH WORK IN THE FIELD OF PSYCHOLOGY

DR REKHA RANI

Made with ❤ on the Notion Press Platform
www.notionpress.com

Dedicated

To all women

Who continue to inspire the world

With their love, compassion

And courage!

To all remarkable women

Whose pursuit of education and career inspire many lives.

With unwavering love, boundless compassion, and

Incredible courage, they redefine possibilities.

May their steps illuminate an equitable

Future and ignite change for all

Contents

A STUDY OF
SELF CONCEPT, SEX ROLE AND MARITAL ADJUSTMENT AMONG EMPLOYED AND UNEMPLOYED EDUCATED WOMEN

Thesis
Submitted for the degree of
DOCTOR OF PHILOSOPHY IN PSYCHOLOGY
FACULTY OF SOCIAL SCIENCES

Supervisor
Dr. Meena Shrivastava
Reader & Head, Dept. of Psychology S.S.L.N.T., Mahila College
Dhanbad
A P.G. Unit of VBU, Hazaribagh

Submitted by
Rekha Rani

Department of Psychology
Vinoba Bhave University, Hazaribagh
2001

Foreword

In an era where the empowerment of women stands as a cornerstone of societal progress, the importance of education and its impact on the lives of women cannot be overstated. This book, dedicated to the insightful exploration of educated women, arrives as a timely and essential contribution.

The pages that follow delve into a subject that resonates deeply with the contemporary world. As societies evolve, the empowerment of women through education becomes not only a choice but a necessity. In this context, the significance of this book cannot be emphasized enough.

The exploration of the experiences, challenges, and triumphs of educated women encapsulates the very essence of societal transformation. It is a narrative of resilience, growth, and the remarkable strides taken towards gender equality.

As we navigate a complex global landscape, where voices clamor for change and progress, this book serves as a beacon of knowledge. It illuminates the path towards understanding the intricate dynamics that shape the lives of educated women and their role in shaping the future.

This book stands as a testament to the power of education and the indomitable spirit of women who, armed with knowledge, contribute to building a better world for themselves and for all.

In acknowledging the need of our times, this book underscores the truth that the empowerment of educated women is not just a concept; it is the cornerstone of progress.

Ashish Karan
Ex Director, The Carlyle Group
PGDM IIM Ahmedabad, B Tech IIT Kharagpur.

In Todays time where women are emerging as trailblazers across various spheres, this book is a beacon of knowledge that illuminates their multifaceted experiences. With a keen eye on empirical evidence, the author unveils the layers that shape a woman's sense of self and her interactions within the intricate web of personal and societal relationships.

This book is an invitation to explore the transformative potential of education and employment in the lives of women. It offers not only an understanding of their evolving self-concepts but also a glimpse into the dynamic dance of marital adjustments and the evolution of gender roles.

As we engage with this thought-provoking narrative, let us acknowledge the significance of this endeavor in contributing to the discourse on women's empowerment and the evolving landscape of gender dynamics. This book, with its rich insights and comprehensive analysis, is a testament to the indomitable spirit of women and their ability to shape and reshape the world around them.

Chandni Sahay
Ex Bank officer, Union Bank of India, ICICI Bank
Engineer, Cummins College of Engineering, Pune

In the realm of contemporary society, the dynamics of womanhood have transcended traditional boundaries, embracing new roles, challenges, and aspirations. Within these pages lies a compelling exploration, aptly titled "Unveiling Dimensions: The Psychological Landscape of Modern Women." This book serves guiding us through the intricate interplay of education, career pursuits, self-concept, marital dynamics, and evolving gender roles.

At a juncture where women's voices resonate with unprecedented vigor, this work takes us on an expedition of understanding and empathy. Rooted in rigorous research, it unravels the effects of education and professional engagement on the multifaceted dimensions of a woman's life.

From self-discovery to partnership dynamics, this book shines a light on the profound impact of education and employment on the psychological makeup of women. Through its nuanced analysis, it offers a panoramic view of how these elements influence self-perception, relationships, and societal roles.

As we immerse ourselves in these pages, let us recognize the significance of this journey. The author's dedication to unraveling complexities and unveiling truths exemplifies a commitment to empowering women with knowledge and self-awareness.

May this book serve as a guidepost for scholars, thinkers, and individuals seeking insight into the evolving paradigms of womanhood. It is an ode to the resilient spirit of women as they navigate a world that continually transforms, and a testament to the enduring power of education and professional fulfillment.

Smita Sahay

Editor-in-Chief, Usawa Literary Review

Somatic therapist, Calm Space

Indian School of Business

In today's rapidly evolving society, understanding the intricate fabric of psychological dimensions has never been more crucial. "An Exploration into the Psychological Makeup of Today's Women: The Impact of Education and Employment on Self-Concept, Marital Adjustment, and Sex Roles" is an exceptional literary endeavor that delves deep into these very dimensions. As we traverse through the pages of this remarkable book, we find a embarking on a journey of self-discovery of todays women.

I will recommend this to all individuals looking to comprehend the nuanced interplay between education, employment, self-perception, marital dynamics, and gender roles

Keshav Ratan

Graduate, IIT Kharagpur

In the tapestry of human existence, the threads of womanhood have woven a narrative of strength, adaptability, and transformation. "Resonance: Mapping the Psyche of the Modern Woman" invites us to embark on an illuminating journey that traverses the realms of education, vocations, self-identity, partnership dynamics, and the evolving tapestry of gender roles.

In an era defined by unprecedented strides in gender equality and self-realization, this book emerges as a guiding star, shedding light on the intricate mosaic of contemporary womanhood. It artfully decodes the impact of education and professional engagements on the psychological landscapes of these remarkable individuals.

Beyond the mere dissemination of information, this book beckons us to introspect, reflect, and reimagine. Through meticulous exploration, it uncovers the layers that shape self-perception, alter relationship dynamics, and redefine societal roles, inviting readers to question preconceived notions and embrace new paradigms.

The pages ahead carry not just words, but an invitation to engage in a dialogue that bridges the gap between research and reality. It is a testament to the author's unwavering dedication, a mirror to the collective experiences of modern women, and a compass guiding us toward a more equitable and empathetic world.

As we embark on this expedition, let us acknowledge the uniqueness of this endeavor — a literary tapestry that weaves empirical insights with the aspirations, challenges, and dreams of women in the 21st century.

Ashish Kumar
Published Author

In the intricate weaving of society, the evolution of women's roles has been a testament to the relentless march of progress. The narrative of their journey, as depicted in the book "The Psychological Dynamics of Modern Womanhood: Navigating Education, Career, Marriage, and Identity," offers an insightful exploration of the multi-faceted lives they lead today.

In the annals of time, women have transcended societal constraints and emerged as powerful agents of change. This book delves into the psychological makeup of contemporary women, unravelling the impact of education and career pursuits on their self-concept, marital dynamics, and ever-evolving sex roles. As we embark on this journey through the pages, we are confronted with narratives that are both illuminating and empowering.

The effect of education and employment on women's self-concept is a topic that resonates with the very essence of their empowerment. Education is the beacon that kindles the fires of aspiration, igniting the desire to explore uncharted territories. In these pages, we encounter stories of women who have harnessed education as a tool to transcend boundaries, discovering newfound confidence and a robust sense of self. The book delves into the intricate interplay between education, self-esteem, and self-efficacy, showing us that when women are equipped with knowledge, they become architects of their own destinies.

The narrative doesn't stop at the classroom door; it delves into the corridors of the workplace where women carve their niches as professionals. The stories here echo the profound impact of careers on self-concept. The pride of accomplishment, the camaraderie of collaboration, and the challenges that pave the way to growth are all intricately woven into the fabric of each woman's journey.

Marriage, a sacred institution in many cultures, undergoes transformation as women straddle their careers and personal lives. This book dares to explore the complexities of marital dynamics, delving into the intricacies of partnership, compromise, and the pursuit of equality. The stories shared here uncover the delicate balance between companionship and individual growth, inviting readers to ponder the beauty of harmonizing two unique narratives within the institution of marriage.

Sex roles, once rigidly defined, are now fluid and ever-evolving. The book traverses the terrain of shifting gender roles, underscoring how modern women navigate the intersections of tradition and progress. These narratives articulate how women, as they embrace diverse roles, challenge the norms of yesteryears while building bridges towards an egalitarian society.

As you journey through the following chapters, let these stories serve as mirrors reflecting the aspirations, struggles, and triumphs of the modern woman. The words within these pages are a testament to the resilience, strength, and endless possibilities that define womanhood in the present day. May this book inspire dialogue, encourage reflection, and pave the way for continued progress, fostering an environment where women can unfold their potential unhindered and unapologetically.

Shatrughan Sharan
Retired Head Surveyor
Central CoalField Ltd.

Within the kaleidoscope of societal transformation, the stories of women have emerged as vibrant threads, weaving tales of empowerment, growth, and self-discovery. As we embark upon the intellectual journey offered by the book "Unveiling the Psyche of Modern Women: Exploring the Impact of Education, Career, Marriage, and Gender Roles," we are invited to explore the nuanced dimensions of women's lives in today's world.

The intricate interplay of education and career within the lives of women holds a captivating resonance. This book unveils the layers of transformation that education brings forth, as it shapes not only the pursuit of knowledge but also the very essence of selfhood. Within these pages, we encounter narratives that illuminate the empowerment that springs from the acquisition of knowledge. The stories told here echo the empowerment women derive from education, as they nurture their intellectual passions, challenge conventions, and reimagine their identities.

The professional sphere, once predominantly male-dominated, now bears the mark of women's prowess. The narratives within this book traverse the terrain of careers, showcasing the intricate dance between ambition and personal growth. The stories unfold like a tapestry, weaving tales of determination, resilience, and the formidable impact of women in the workforce. Through their experiences, we gain insight into the dynamic evolution of women's self-concept, sculpted by their professional achievements and the challenges they navigate.

Marriage, a cornerstone of societal fabric, is reimagined through the lens of modernity. This book delves into the complexities of marital dynamics, exploring the intricate balance between shared dreams and individual aspirations. The narratives unfurl stories of women who redefine partnerships, embracing equality, communication, and the pursuit of personal growth within the sacred bond of matrimony.

In the landscape of gender roles, seismic shifts have dismantled traditional boundaries. The stories within this book resonate with the evolving narratives of modern women who transcend the confines of societal expectations. The exploration of gender roles ventures into uncharted territories, spotlighting women who defy convention, shaping their destinies on their own terms. Through these tales, we glimpse the mosaic of strength, courage, and resilience that characterizes the modern woman.

As you delve into the following chapters, allow these narratives to be a conduit for introspection, dialogue, and celebration. The words contained herein are an ode to the spirit of the modern woman, a tribute to her unwavering determination, and an affirmation of her ability to forge her path. May this book serve as a source of inspiration, fostering conversations that enrich our collective understanding and fuel the ongoing journey towards equality and empowerment.

Pramila Sharan
Ex- Principal of Women college
Ramgarh, Jharkhand

Preface

I hold a Ph.D. in Psychology, a PGDM in Human Resource and a Certificate degree in Child Counselling and Guidance. I have written widely in Hindi newspapers and books. I am the co-creator of MA Psychology (Hindi) course material for Nalanda Open University, Patna. I have taught MBA, MA and BA classes in reputed colleges in Patna and Lucknow. My Ph.D research work titled - 'To study the Self Concept, Sex Role and Marital adjustment among employed and unemployed educated women' is an extensive study of gender role adjustment and its effects on the psyche of Indian women.

I have also worked as Chief of Psychologist at a mental health startup, AccioHealth, where my role involved a 360 degree approach, including testing and counselling of patients and training of young psychologists in the team. I have published a number of books. I am an avid blogger. I share short stories, poems and psychology related articles on my blog.

Acknowledgements

With immense gratitude, I wish to express my heartfelt acknowledgment to the Almighty, whose boundless grace and guidance have been my constant companions throughout this journey. This endeavor would not have been possible without the invaluable contributions of numerous women who wholeheartedly participated in my research, sharing their insights and experiences.

I extend my deepest appreciation to every individual who played a role, no matter how small, in the realization of this work in its final book form. The journey from a thesis to a published book is laden with challenges, and it is with a sense of profound thankfulness that I recognize those who stood by me during this transformative process.

To the mentors, friends, and family members who offered unwavering encouragement and support, I am truly grateful. Each word penned, each page written, and each idea conceptualized has been infused with the collective energy of those who believed in this endeavor.

In closing, I offer my sincere thanks to the Almighty, the women who generously shared their stories, and every individual who contributed to the fulfillment of this vision. Your involvement has not only enriched this work but has also strengthened my belief in the power of collaboration and shared knowledge.

With heartfelt thanks,
Dr Rekha Rani

Prologue

Topic Of My Thesis -To study the self-concept, sex-role and marital adjustment among educated, employed and unemployed women. (Vinoba Bhave University,Hazaribag, Jharkhand India)

The journey that led to the creation of this thesis spanned nearly five years – a span of time marked by dedication, perseverance, and unwavering commitment. This endeavor, at its core, sought to unravel the intricate layers of the modern woman's psyche, a pursuit that was far from ordinary.

Gathering data from a diverse group of 400 educated women, both employed and non-employed, proved to be a herculean feat. The path was not without its challenges; many women hesitated at the outset, wary of delving into the realm of personal experiences. However, their reservations were quelled when the realization dawned that this study held profound implications for women of today, shaping their journeys in ways yet unforeseen.

As an educated woman myself, I embarked on this quest fueled by a desire to unearth insights that could illuminate the path ahead. The significance of this research, born out of an intrinsic curiosity, became ever more apparent as the days turned into months and the months into years.

This thesis stands as a testament to the collective spirit of those who contributed their time, thoughts, and experiences. It embodies the relentless pursuit of knowledge and the courage to confront the complexities that lie within. It is a journey marked by introspection, understanding, and the pursuit of a deeper truth.

As these pages unfold, they bear witness to the stories of women who shared their journeys with honesty and vulnerability. In every line, every statistic, and every revelation, lies the heartbeat of a collective narrative that seeks to empower, educate, and inspire.

May this thesis serve as a guiding light, casting its radiance on the path of every woman, as we collectively journey towards a more enlightened and inclusive future.

This book stands as the culmination of my cherished dream project. Originally recognized with an award back in 2001, this thesis has held within it the seeds of a long-awaited aspiration. Its transformation into a published work has been a journey of anticipation and persistence.

The significance of this achievement cannot be understated, as it marks the realization of a vision nurtured over the years. From the moment of its initial recognition to its eventual publication, this endeavor has been an ardent pursuit, driven by passion and dedication.

As the pages of this book come to life, they carry with them not just the culmination of research and insights but also the essence of unwavering commitment. The journey from a celebrated thesis to a published book has been one of evolution and growth, embodying the spirit of resilience and the power of perseverance.

In every word, every chapter, and every concept explored, this book represents the fulfillment of a dream that has been nurtured over time. It is a testament to the enduring pursuit of knowledge and the fulfillment of a promise made to oneself.

With heartfelt satisfaction,
Dr Rekha Rani

Dr. (Mrs) Meena Shrivastava
    M. A. (Gold Medalist), Ph.D. (P.U.)
    Reader in Psychology

S. S. L. N. T. Women's College
DHANBAD-826001
HAZARIBAGH, BIHAR

Certificate

This is to certify that Mre. Rekha Rani has completed her original work on the topic "A study of self-concept, sex role and marital adjustment among educated employed and unemployed women" under my supervision satisfactorily leading to the award of Ph. D. Degree under Vinoba Bhave University. Hazaribagh vide Registration No. Ph.DIS. So 00221196.

The contents of the thesis are original contribution of the author and did not form a basis for the award of any previous degree to her or any body else to best of my knowledge.

The instant research work shall benefit in adding knowledge in the field of women's study.

The thesis fedfills the requèrement for the award of Ph. D. Degree of VINOBA BHAVE UNVERSITY. HAZARIBAGH and is fit for submission. In habit and character Mrs. Rekha Rani is a fit person for the award of Ph. D. Degree.

At the outset I express my deep sense of gratitude to Dr. (Mrs.) Meena Shrivastava, Reader & Head, P. G. Deptt. of Psychology, S.S.L.N.T. Mahila College, Dhanbad, Vinoba Bhave University, Hazaribagh, for extending her ever inspiring guidance, encouragement and counsel, without which it would not have been possible for me to complete the present thesis. I owe a debt of gratitude to Dr. Enayatullah, Head, P. G. Department of Psychology, Vinoba Bhave University, Hazaribagh for his valuable co- operation and guidance.

I wish to express my sincere thanks to Prof. Dr. A. J. Prakash who has been kind enough to provide me his experienced advice and inspiration to me for completing the job. Miss Priyanka deserves my heartiest thanks for helping me in many ways.

I am thankful to Mr. Lalan Prasad, I.O.C. Dhanbad and Mrs. Nanda Singh, I.O.C. Patna who helped me a lot to shape the present work by providing me with recent studies available on internet. I am thankful to Mr. Jamil, Manager, Informatics Computer Institute. He helped me in data coding and processing through computer. I also thank Mrs. Rumna Bhattacharya and Mr. Rajnish Kumar for their help.

Thanks are also due to the Librarian and all the staff of A. N. Sinha Institute of Social Studies for their kind co-operation during my research work.

I thankfully acknowledge the blessings, inspiration, love, co-operation and encouragement of my parents, in-laws, brothers, sisters and friends without whom the present work would not have been the light of the day.

1 AM indebted to my husband Mr. Adhar Kumar, Senior Manager, Punjab National Bank whose inspiration has all along been with me during the completion of the present work. I can not miss to thank my daughters Smita and Chandni for their whole hearted co-operation. I am equally grateful to all those women who have given their time, energy in answering the questionnaire of the present study and the date which is the basis of present research work.

Last but not the least I extend my thanks to Mr. B. D. Mandal, Senior. Steno, CMRI, Dhanbad for typing the thesis efficiently. I am also thankful to all those who directly and indirectly helped me in completion of the thesis.

Rekha Rani

CHAPTER – I Introduction: Towards equality

The Indian Women

In the past few decades, women in India have achieved a new status with the addition of the role of working women to their existing roles. Various studies have shown that the attitudes of educated women, particularly educated working women, have considerably changed, especially with regard to marriage, family, and status.

The role of Indian women is full of diversity and contradictions, varying across ethnic groups and socio-economic levels. Earlier, women were primarily associated with managing the internal interface of the social system.

Throughout the centuries, women in India have silently maintained the permanence and stability of society's cultural institutions and the continuities and consistencies of its ethos. In this context, women have been regarded as the virtue holders of society, leading lives of various roles, including employed women.

Today, this aspect of women's lives has acquired a new dimension. Educated and armed with knowledge and skills, women enter formal work settings, disconnecting themselves from their traditional social structures and networks of relationships. Like their male counterparts, they venture into the world of occupations, careers, professions, competition, and achievements, striving to create a space where they can experience themselves and be accepted as autonomous beings. They feel compelled to discover and identify their personal resources, envision a life beyond marriage and the defined social structures, and encounter the opportunity to create a world beyond the horizon, which could become their own. They visualize themselves playing a role beyond the micro-social, encompassing the dimension of a synthesizing human existence.

Contemporary Indian women find themselves caught between the traditional past and a modern future, inspired by their dreams and aspirations, yet uncertain of their self-worth and competencies.

This book is based on research work focusing on the lives of educated, married, employed, and unemployed women. It attempts to shed light on the changing position of educated, married women in society, with a special focus on their self-concept, gender roles, and marital adjustments.

Today, work holds deep meaning in the lives of women. They are breaking through the hard shell of traditionalism to fulfill various psychological and personal needs, such as the need for recognition, emotional responses, personal experiences, security, novelty of experiences, economic freedom, and a sense of creativity.

It is important to understand how successfully educated, married, and employed women have been able to achieve and maintain harmony and happiness in their married and family lives. The study aims to explore the changes that the added role has brought into their lives and to determine their self-concept and gender roles, which play a vital role in their psycho-social makeup. It also focuses on studying the adjustments in their marriages.

Due to technological transitions in the economic processes and the emergence of the industrial era in India, a new process of work ethics, technology, and consequently, a new lifestyle has been introduced. Education is now available to all citizens of India post-independence. Through education, women have entered various fields such as fashion, teaching, medicine, administrative services, law, engineering, politics, and the growing business organizations and manufacturing industries. They have carved out new roles for themselves. The role of Indian women has undergone dramatic and drastic changes, affecting family life and marital adjustments. Standing at this threshold, women are encountering an identity crisis for the first time.

In essence, today's women embrace the role of being creators of a new heritage, rather than mere inheritors. Women in this space must transcend the biosocial fragmentation of male-female, man-woman, and masculine-feminine roles, integrating them in a wholesome manner into a single identity - a human identity.

Education - Influencing the Behavior of Women

Today, rapid changes are taking place in society. The industrial revolution, urbanization, recently acquired legal and political rights, education, advanced technology, birth control, advancements in mass media, job opportunities, and new opportunities for female education are significant recent changes influencing the attitudes of educated women in India. Concurrently, concepts such as gender equality, women's liberation, and human rights have made them more conscious of their rights.

Over the past half-century, the proportion of educated women has significantly increased. With a rise in the number of educated women taking up employment in various fields and capacities, there is a noticeable trend of women entering the workforce due to higher levels of educational qualifications. Education is leaving a positive impact on all aspects of life.

Education is leading to considerable changes in the attitudes of young educated women. Instead of being tradition-directed, they are transitioning to being more inner-directed. They are gradually developing detraditionalized life patterns and lifestyles, with their attitudes and values becoming more egalitarian. With this new emergence of educational trends, women are developing more balanced personalities filled with confidence and a positive sense of self.

Self-Concept (Who Am I?)

Definition and Importance - Self-concept encompasses all aspects of one's being and experiences that are perceived in awareness by individuals. According to Burn (1977), "Self-concept is a composite image of what we think we are, what we think others think of us, and what we aspire to be."

The most significant and current interpretation of human personality is rooted in self-concept theory. Throughout recorded history, humans have sought to understand the reasons behind their behavior to establish a sense of identity.

The term "self-concept" originated in the twentieth century but is now highlighted as a crucial focal point in individual experiences due to its centrality, primacy, and continuity in all aspects of behavior, mediating as both a stimulus and a response.

While a concept of self is implied in Freud's work (1936, 1964), the emphasis on the id functioning overshadowed the ego, and the self-concept construct never became explicit enough.

Neo-Freudians like Fromm (1941) firmly established the self-concept as a significant construct in the study of human behavior.

Jung (1951) believed that the self represents an equilibrium between the conscious (ego) and unconscious levels but did not emphasize it as central to his theories.

Adler (1927) viewed humans as conscious beings usually aware of their reasons for behavior, capable of organizing and guiding their actions with complete awareness of the implications for their own self-realization.

According to field theory by Lewin (1936), the self-concept lies within the life space region as a core area in an individual's psychological universe.

Raimy (1948) expanded this self-concept from a perceptual frame of reference into the clinical realm, defining self-concept as a learned perceptual system functioning as an object in the perceptual field.

Allport (1961) described the self-concept as something of immediate awareness, portraying it as the central, private region of our life, existing in our consciousness (a concept broader than self) and in our personality (a concept broader than personality). Thus, it seems to vanish from awareness, leaving no self-awareness whatsoever.

The role of humanistic psychologists is crucial in the field of self-concept. According to humanistic psychologists, self-concept denotes an individual's conception of the kind of person they are. The self-concept is one's image of oneself.

Rogers (1951) explained self-concept as "an organized configuration of self-perceptions admissible to awareness."

Rogers (1959) defined it as the organized, consistent conceptual characteristics of "I" or "ME" related to perceptions of others, various life aspects, and the value attached to these perceptions. The ideal self is introduced into the theory as "the self-concept which the individual would most like to possess and holds in high regard for oneself."

Shavelson et al. (1976) described self-concept as a person's perception based on behaviors of themselves, found through personal experiences, interpretation of one's environment, evaluation by significant others, self-concept, and attributions for one's behavior.

In a study by Tajfel and Turner (1985), it was stated that an individual's self-concept is derived from social categories to which they perceive themselves as belonging.

At the annual meeting of the Academy of Management in August 1995, Leonard, Beauvais, and Scholl (1995) stated that the self-concept is the underlying force that energizes, directs, and sustains behavior, serving as a source of motivation and a unifying framework. According to them, one's concept of self comprises four interrelated self-perceptions:

The perceived self

The ideal self

One's self-esteem

A set of social identities

Each of these elements plays a crucial role in understanding how the self-concept relates to energizing, directing, and sustaining psychosocial behaviors. In research in Social Psychology, Greenwald and Poratkani (1984); Schlenker (1980); Markus and Wurf (1987) have conceptualized the self-concept as a multifaceted phenomenon consisting of a set of images, schemas, and prototypes.

Therefore, the self-concept is both a perception and a concept around which values are internalized from the culture and regulate behaviors. The self-concept remains relatively consistent over time and situations, leading to relatively consistent behavioral patterns.

Knowledge and evaluation are two fundamental elements of the self-concept. Knowledge is closely tied to the self-concept, acquired through education, teachers, and peer groups. Evaluation is based on this acquired knowledge. The evaluative loading of the self-concept is learned and can change in direction and weighting based on other learning experiences encountered. For example, a person may view themselves as a bright student based on academic performance and feedback, but this self-evaluation can fluctuate as significant others in their peer group begin to emphasize other behaviors, such as athleticism. As time passes, one might discover that academic success alone is not the sole criterion for happiness or success in life, leading to a change in this weighting while maintaining a positive self-evaluation. Self-evaluation is context-specific and not fixed; it varies based on each specific context. Evaluative significance is derived from the surrounding culture, where many evaluations become normative. A positive self-concept is equated with positive self-evaluation, self-respect, self-esteem, self-acceptance, while a negative self-concept is associated with negative self-evaluation, self-loathing, feelings of inferiority, and a lack of personal worth and self-acceptance. These terms carry connotations of each other and are used interchangeably by various authors like Wylic (1968); Coopersmith (1967).

Structre of Self : In a review, Markus and Wurf (1987) stated that the most dramatic advancement in the last decade of research on the self-concept can be found in its structure and content. The concept of self is composed of four interrelated self-perceptions:

The Perceived Self: William James (1890) saw the self as consisting of whatever the individual views as belonging to themselves. This includes a material, social, and spiritual self. The material self encompasses perceptions of one's own body, family, and possessions. The social self includes how others perceive the individual, while the spiritual self involves perceptions of emotions and desires. Kihlstrom, Cantor, and their associates (1988, 1987) suggested that individuals perceive themselves in terms of traits, values, attributes, experiences, thoughts, actions, physical appearance, demographic attributes, and various dispositions. Gecas (1982) asserts that the contents of the self-concept consist of perceptions of social and personal identities, traits, attributes, and possessions. Self-perceptions are shaped through interactions, attitude formation, attitude change (Ajzen and Fishbein, 1980), and self-attribution (Jones and Bayley, 1950).

The Ideal Self: While the perceived self describes the set of perceptions individuals hold about their actual traits, competencies, and values, the ideal self represents the traits, competencies, and values an individual would like to possess (Rogers, 1959). This view of the ideal self aligns with Schlenker's (1980) concept of the "idealized image." As individuals interact with reference groups, they receive feedback. If the feedback is positive and unconditional, the individual internalizes the traits, competencies, and values important to that reference group. In such cases, the individual becomes inner-directed, using these internalized standards to measure their own successes and failures. Internalized competencies and values serve as the foundation for the ideal self (Higgins, Klain, and Strauman, 1978) and as an internal standard for behavior (Bandura, 1986). The establishment of the ideal self depends on a mix of external (other-directed) and internal (inner-directed) standards, influenced by an individual's orientation to the world (Reisman, 1961). Gottfredson's (1981) perspective on individual and social achievement motives aligns with this conceptualization.

Social Identities

According to Ashforth and Mael (1989), social identification is a process by which individuals classify themselves and others into different social categories. This classification process serves the functions of segmenting and ordering the social environment, enabling individuals to locate or define themselves within that social context. Social identities, therefore, encompass aspects of an individual's self-concept that derive from the social categories to which they perceive themselves as belonging (Tajfel and

Turner, 1985).

Individuals establish social identities through their involvement with reference groups in various social situations. These social identities link individuals to specific reference groups, which establish role expectations and norms guiding behavior within each social identity.

The determination of the relevant attributes that comprise an identity is not fixed; rather, it results from an ongoing interaction process between individuals, subgroups, and members of the relevant reference group. This definition and redefinition of identity are constant processes (Bandura, 1986; Markus and Wurf, 1987).

Self-Esteem

Self-esteem represents the evaluative component of an individual's self-concept and personality traits (Gergen, 1971; Rosenberg, 1965). It depends on the perceived distance between the ideal self, the attitudinal component, and the perceived self.

Korman (1970) identifies three types of self-esteem:

Chronic self-esteem: This relatively persistent personality trait or dispositional state consistently occurs across various situations.

Task-specific self-esteem: It pertains to an individual's self-perception of competence in a particular task or job.

Socially influenced self-esteem: This type of self-esteem is influenced by the expectations of others.

Hurlock (1974) provides a more specific definition of self-concept, emphasizing its structural components. The self-concept comprises three major components:

Perceptual component: Similar to the physical self-concept, it includes the image of one's appearance, attractiveness, and the appropriateness of one's body in terms of sex. Different body parts also play a role.

Conceptual component: This aspect relates to the psychological self-concept, encompassing an individual's origin, abilities, disabilities, and personality traits.

Attitudinal component: Referring to attitudes about present status and future prospects, this component includes feelings of self-worth, self-esteem, beliefs, convictions, values, ideals, aspirations, and commitments.

In summary, the structural definition of self-concept, as presented by Hurlock, underscores its central and inclusive significance for an individual, influencing all behaviors—whether simple or complex.

Development of Self-Concept

According to Cooley (1912), self and society are twin-born, and the notion of a separate and independent ego is an illusion.

Self-concept is a learned behavior, so it can be healthy or unhealthy due to environmental factors, child-rearing practices, school experiences, or peer groups. Sherif and Contril (1947) have cited many instances of gradual self-conception in children. Piaget (195) indicates that initially, infants exist in an undifferentiated state where there are no clear boundaries between their bodies and other objects, between reality and fantasy. However, over time, they begin to distinguish between what is themselves and what is not.

The process of self-concept development never truly ends. It actively unfolds from birth to death as individuals continually discover new potentials within themselves.

Various sources play important roles in self-concept development at different stages of the lifespan, although they do not act independently. These sources are closely interwoven with social living. Feedback and experiences are crucial in shaping self-concept. It is relatively stable, developed, influenced, and reinforced through serial and task feedback, ultimately affecting behavior. Self-concept is a continuous, lifelong developmental process (Filipp, Sigrun & Heide, 1980).

Self-Concept and Relevant Variables

Several factors relate to self-concept. The most influential ones include physical attributes, material possessions, group affiliations, roles, values, interests, wants, and goals (Gesell & Lig, 1949; Staines, 1958).

Expressive, Acognitive, and Cognitive Processes

Understanding the link between self-concept and behavior involves expressive, acognitive, and cognitive processes.

Acognitive Process: This expressive component of self-concept refers to how individuals process information, feedback, and observations. They use the structure of their self-concept to filter incoming information and translate it into action.

Cognitive Models of Behavior: Much of the work on self-concept relies on cognitive models. Many behaviors result from thought processes that are consciously inspected by individuals. However, some behaviors arise from processes not entirely understood or conscious to the individual. Kihlstrom et al. (1987) refer to these aspects of the self as preconscious or subconscious. Self-perceptions of traits, competencies, and values exist as knowledge structures that monitor and control experiences, thoughts, and actions. Some knowledge structures are cognitive and provide data for information processing in social situations, leading to stable behavioral patterns across contexts. Other knowledge structures may be inaccessible under certain conditions.

Self-Concept and Child Rearing Practice

The first five years of a child's life are widely accepted by psychologists as a fundamental period for shaping personality and self-conceptions. Stott (1939) initially discovered the pattern of child-rearing practices that facilitate positive self-concepts. Coopersmith (1967) also indicated that parents' desire for their children to be self-confident is related to self-concept development. According to Coopersmith, positive self-concepts are more likely to emerge when children are treated with respect, provided with well-defined standards, and given reasonable expectations of success. Numerous other studies have yielded similar results. For instance, Medinnus and Curtis (1963) found that children of high self-esteem mothers also tend to have high self-esteem, while children from families with low self-esteem mothers exhibit lower self-esteem. Coopersmith (1967) further explained that fathers of high self-esteem children play a more supportive and active role in child-rearing compared to fathers of low self-esteem children. Watkins (1976) also highlighted a significant relationship between self-esteem and fathers' education, as well as self-esteem and parental conflict.

In child-rearing practices, the family and its environment play a crucial role. A study conducted by Ziller (1973) on Indian children explored cross-cultural differences in self-concept related to family relationships among Asian, Indian, and American children. The extended family environment of Indian children is presumed to have implications for their self-concept. In contrast to American children, Indian children exhibit higher self-esteem, greater social interest, and stronger identification with parents, but a narrower range of identification with others.

Self-Concept and Language

Verbal language plays a vital role in self-concept development. Language symbols form the basis for our conceptions and evaluations of ourselves. The use of pronouns such as "Me," "I," "Mine," and "He" or "Them" distinguishes self from others. Self-awareness becomes increasingly apparent when individuals correctly differentiate between "I," "You," "Mine," and "Yours."

For an infant, their name becomes a crucial linguistic marker. Allport (1961) concluded that hearing one's name repeatedly gradually leads the child to perceive themselves as a distinct and recurring point of reference.

Body Language

Nonverbal communication, or body language, also conveys information about the self and reflects how others perceive us. Argyle's study (1967) revealed that certain nonverbal codes and signs communicate more powerfully than words alone. Abercrombie (1968) similarly emphasized that we communicate with our entire body.

Self-Concept and Feedback from Significant Others

Most personality theorists and researchers agree on the role of children's perception of their significant others. These individuals, who hold importance in a child's life, significantly influence self-concept. Their ability to reduce insecurity, increase or decrease feelings of helplessness, and play a confirming role in self-definition is crucial. Snygg and Combs (1949) have also emphasized the vital effects of how significant others evaluate us. Cooley (1912) and Mead (1934) elaborated on the sources of self-esteem in the early days of self-concept theory. Cooley (1912) famously described the self as perceived through the reflections in the eyes of others, akin to looking through a mirror. Raimy (1948) highlighted what a person believes about themselves as a factor in social comprehension. According to Murphy (1947), it is vitally important to protect children from acquiring an unlovely view of themselves. However, Freclerick (1980) and Muhlenkamp, Ann, Sayles, Judy (1986) discuss the development of self-concept with reference to the importance of individual perception.

All types of self-consciousness are associated with aspects of identity. Cheek, Jonathan, and Briggs, Stephan (1982) found that public self-consciousness was significantly more correlated with personal aspects of identity than social ones. Coleman, Michael (1985) also identified expectations of achievement as an influence on children's perception of their own competence. Extolla, Watkin, David Amile (1982) found a significant correlation between self-concept and their perceptions.

Self-Concept and Influence of Parents and Siblings

Psychologists widely believe that the first five years of a child's life are crucial. Leonoru (1984) discovered that parents' relationship, behavior towards the child, birth order, and other factors facilitate the development of self-concept. As Freud explained, children copy the behavior of their parents through identification (Bandura, Ross, and Ross, 1963a).

The role of fathers and mothers is paramount in rearing and bringing up their children. Helper (1955) found that the degree of likeness or identification with the father was related to the popularity of high school boys. Mothers also assume a prominent role in girls' lives as they grow older (Bayley and Schaefer, 1960). Coopersmith (1967) found that self-esteem was strongly associated with parental attitudes, warmth, and the rules and disciplines imposed by parents on their children.

Self-Concept and Birth Order

Birth order, or the rank of the child in the family, also influences the development of self-concept. Estella, Watkins, David Astilla (1982) compared first-born, last-born, and middle-born female subjects, but no influence of birth order was found in this study. Kindwell, Jeannie (1982), Mills, Griffore, Robert, and Bianchi, Leonard (1984) found that middle-borns have significantly lower self-esteem than first and last-borns.

Self-Concept and Family Structure

The structure of the family, whether it is a joint family or nuclear family, influences personality and self-concept. Other family members, their relationships, behavior, and child-rearing practices all impact the development of self-concept. Ziller (1973) found that Indian children possess high levels of self-esteem due to the joint family structure. However, Sear's (1970) does not support this evidence. According to Sear, in nuclear families, parental care and warmth contribute to children having high self-esteem. Bannon, Jill, and Southern (1980) explored the relationship between the absence of a father in childhood and self-concept but found no significant association. Slater, Elisa, Stewart, Krista, and Linn (1983) discovered that intact, divorced, separated, and reconstituted families have unique and marked impacts on the development of self-concept and the choice of particular objectives.

Slater, Elisa, and Haber, Joel (1984) also found that in parent-separated families, due to conflict, children also experience conflict related to self-concept. Additionally, it was observed that high conflict produced lower levels of self-concept. Rosenthal, David, Peng, Chao Ying, & McMillan (1980) supported this conclusion and found that children from single-parent families had lower self-esteem than those with both parents.

Self-Concept and Physical Self and Body Image

Self-concept plays a central role in human behavior, and changes in self-concept lead to corresponding changes in behavior. Body image involves estimating and evaluating physical attractiveness based on social norms and feedback from significant others. Initially, self-concept is closely tied to body image—an evaluated mental picture of the physical self. Factors such as body build, appearance, and size significantly contribute to understanding a person's self-concept. Secord and Backman (1964) demonstrated that males were most satisfied with their bodies when they were larger, while females tended to be more satisfied if they were shorter. Body image constitutes a considerable and significant part of the overall self-concept, as highlighted by Kretschmer (1925) and Sheldon and Stevens (1942).

Height, weight, complexion, eyesight, and body proportions are closely associated with attitudes and feelings of personal adequacy and acceptability. Staaffieri (1957) noted that stereotypes of behavior are linked to body types. Physical appearance wields significant influence over self-concept. Numerous studies have confirmed the close relationship between attraction, health, height, shape, and self-concept, as discussed by Jegede, Olukayoda, and Bamgboye (Afolabi, 1981).

Self-Concept and Education

The development of self-concept is a lifelong process, and personal educational performance is closely linked to it. Even in school-going children, self-concept remains susceptible to modification. Teachers and peer groups play a major role in shaping self-concept. Teachers, in particular, serve as significant others in a child's self-concept development. Staines (1958) emphasized the importance of education in self-concept development. Subsequent research has explored the significant relationship between low self-concept and academic underachievement, as highlighted by Fink (1962). Jones and Grieneeks (1970) found that academic achievement and self-concept positively influence each other. Simon and Simon (1975) also reported a significant relationship between self-esteem and standardized academic achievement for both sexes. In another investigation focused on the relationship between self-concept and school achievement, Stennes and Katzenmeyer (1976) obtained overwhelming evidence supporting the positive association between self-concept and academic performance. Caslyn and Kenny (1977) analyzed data from a longitudinal study of 556 adolescents, comparing the self-enhancement model with the skill development approach. Self-enhancement theory suggests that self-concept variables impact academic performance levels. Leonard Gregry Eugene (1990) found that self-concept changes with age, and boys and girls did not differ significantly in their math aptitudes. However, girls expressed more positive attitudes toward school and verbal items.

The organizational structure of schools significantly supports self-concept development. Teachers and teacher-pupil relationships play crucial roles in this regard. Thomas (1974) acknowledged the importance of teacher-pupil relationships. In a study by Cohen and Cohen (1974) involving 801 final-year primary children, those with a low self-concept of their ability showed greater dislike for areas of the curriculum offered to both pupils and teachers compared to children with a high self-concept of ability.

Self-Concept of Educated Women and Adolescence

Research on the self-concept of educated women, particularly Indian women, remains scarce. However, recent interest from psycho-social scientists has led to some exploration in this field. In a study by Rapopart, Tamari, Grab-Yone, and Penso Anal (1995), it was reported that women's gender religiosity, subjectivity in religion, and other factors can be influenced by the education system. They found that in Israel, traditional Jewish self-conception among women is filtered through educational practices.

In another recent study, Monck Elizabeth, Graham Philip, Richman Naomi, and Dobbs Rebecca (1994) discovered that the transition from school to future education significantly influences self-concept in teenage girls. Cardoza's study (1991) revealed that daughters of educated mothers were more likely to attend college themselves and have better self-concept. However, Holz-Ebeling Friederike and Hanset Sabine (1993) arrived at a different conclusion. According to them, co-education has a negative academic impact on choices and self-concepts, shedding light on gender inequality. Gustafson Sigrid B, Staltin Hakani, and Magnusson David (1988) noted that education-oriented achievement serves as a significant and valid indicator of sex role orientation.

In a more recent study by Li Xiaodong (1997), self-concept was found to be a multidimensional and hierarchical structure. The frame of reference plays a crucial role in forming academic self-concept. Academic achievement is substantially correlated with academic self-concept, less correlated with general self-concept, and almost not correlated with non-academic self-concept. These studies collectively highlight the importance of education and related factors in self-concept development.

Self-Concept and Adolescence

The correlation between self-concept and adolescence is widely accepted. This period is marked by psychological and physiological maturation, making it a crisis period for adolescents. Simmons, Rosenberg, and Rosenberg (1973) concluded that self-image disturbance occurs during early adolescence. Albam Metcalfe (1978) found no overall difference in self-concepts between adolescent boys and girls. However, when comparing scores from primary and secondary school (same students), it was observed that the scores for children with high self-concept decreased significantly. Colman (1974) discovered that some teenagers struggle with identity problems, while others do not. Jones and Bayley (1950) studied significant differences between two groups: most late and most early maturing boys. Similarly, Mussen and Jones (1957) found that early matures were self-confident and detached, whereas slow development manifested as insecurity and dependence on adults, often reflected in attention-seeking behavior. Engle (1959) identified relatively stable self-concept between ages 13 and 15, as well as at 17 years. Erikson (1968) described adolescence as a period of self-diffusion. Damion, William, and Hart, Daniel (1982) reviewed literature on adolescent self-concept, providing a descriptive account and model of self-understanding development from infancy to childhood. Ellis, Drummond, Gehman, and Ketzenmeyer (1980) explored identity development and the structure of self-concept in adolescence. They found that reconciling physical growth and strong sexual motivations with cultural demands significantly influences self-concept boundaries around age 16. Jogawar (1982) observed stable self-concept in adolescent males peaking at 14 years, while in females, it occurred at 16 years. Abramowitz, Robert H., Peterson Anne, and Schulenberg John (1984) found that early adolescence leads to complex development of self-image in both sexes. However, Jerome and Flahaty John (1981) presented contrasting results, emphasizing continuity and stability in adolescent development. Kato, Takakatsu, and Takagi (1980) found that regardless of age and sex,

Self-Concept and Anxiety

The adolescent period, often considered a crisis period, plays a crucial role not only in evaluating present self-identity but also in shaping future identity. Anxiety, as a disturbed mental state, negatively affects self-concept (Lipsitt 1958; Thompson 1974; Kureshi Afzal, Husain, Akbar 1979; Mitchell 1959; Lamp 1968).

Geist, Charles, and Hemrick Theresa (1983) also found a significant negative correlation between anxiety and self-concept. Davis, Stephan, Bremer, Sarah, Anderson, Brencho, and Tramill (1983) reported a negative relationship between anxiety and self-esteem, while both male and female subjects showed a significant positive relationship between self-esteem and ego strength.

Self-Concept and Health

Physical or mental illness significantly influences personality and self-concept. Regarding mental illness, it is well-established that anxiety and depression are negatively associated with self-concept. Kureshi Afzal, Husain Akbar (1979), Brockner, Joel, and Wallnav Larry (1981), and Hill (1968) all noted a decrease in self-esteem during depression. Wilson, Allam, and Krane Richard (1980) confirmed the hypothesis that positive, negative, or neutral evaluations of health would lead to significant differences in self-esteem levels.

Good physical and mental health consistently contributes to better self-concept. Woods, Nancy, Lentz Martha, and Mitchell Ellen (1993) found that women experiencing less stress were better educated and had a more positive self-concept compared to those engaging in health-damaging behaviors. Reviere, Rebecca, and Eberstein Isaac (1993) concluded in their study on the "effects of marriage and work roles" that better health and self-concept were associated with a lower risk of coronary heart problems in educated working women. Costello Elizabeth (1991) explored the relationship between mental/physical health in educated, married, and employed women, finding that employment did not significantly affect the risk of depression.

Self-Concept and Neuroticism

Neuroticism refers to incorrect functioning of a person's nervous system or psyche, leading to deviating behavior from normalcy. Janet (1893), Charcot (1877), Freud (1917), Adler (1956), and Eysenck (1961) have each attempted to explain neuroticism in their own ways, acknowledging that it represents a distinct personality pattern separate from normal and psychotic personalities.

It is now widely accepted that there exists a negative correlation between self-concept and neuroticism. Kureshi, Akbar, Afzal, and Husain (1979) found an interrelationship between neuroticism and self-concept. Similarly, Brockner, Joel, and Wallnav Larry (1981) reported a negative correlation between self-concept and neuroticism. Alexander, Kaslow, Rehn, Nadine, Lynn, and Siegel (1984) observed that depressed individuals had lower self-concept. A study by Srivastava (1989) on Indian women—divorced, separated, widowed, unmarried, and married—also revealed a negative correlation between self-concept and neuroticism are negatively correlated.

Self-concept and Place of Residence

The place where one resides significantly influences self-concept due to its positive or negative environment. Urban, rural, and metropolitan areas all play crucial roles in shaping and determining an individual's self-concept. The advantages and facilities available in a particular place of residence contribute to this development.

For instance, Edeburn and Gipp (1978) found that students living in Indian reservations had better self-concept compared to those residing in small cities. Similarly, Reck and Una (1980) discovered that rural students generally scored lower in self-concept, regardless of their achievement level.

Self-concept and Socio-Economic Status (SES)

Socio-economic status, which can be categorized into high, middle, and low groups, also significantly impacts self-concept. A person's decision to work is influenced not only by their personality but also by the SES background of their family. When a wife has a career, economic responsibilities are shared between spouses. Hong Sung Mook (1982) supported the idea that socio-economic status is closely related to self-concept. Brown and John (1984), along with Stone and Bernice (1984), highlighted the connection between SES and academic achievement. Low-income youth often face challenges that negatively affect their self-concept. Rao (1978), Drummond, Robert, and Walter (1980), and Bledose and Joseph (1981) all found significant relationships between SES and self-concept. Bledose and Joseph (1981) even hypothesized that economic status is the best predictor of self-concept and provided supportive evidence.

In the Indian context, Sinh Gangawar Hari (1982) discovered that individuals with average or middle socio-economic status had higher self-esteem than those with low status.

Self-concept and Gender

An individual's self-concept is significantly influenced by how they believe others perceive them. Snadocosky and Belkin (1964) emphasized the relationship between self-concept and perceived external judgments. Festinger (1954) introduced the theory of social comparison feedback and appraisal, which positively impacts self-concept. Cultural norms, gender stereotypes, and child-rearing practices contribute to the development of self-concept. Unfortunately, girl children are often considered disadvantaged from an early age, receiving less importance and appraisal compared to male children. This societal bias suppresses self-concept development in female children.

However, studies have shown varying results. Tolar, Kelly, and Stebbin (1976) found that the relationship between self-attitudes and acceptance of others is stronger for women than for men. Some studies suggest that boys have more positive self-concepts than girls during adolescence (Connell et al., 1975; Smith, 1975). On the other hand, Fein et al. (1975) reported that girls experience more role conflict and consequently have lower self-esteem than boys. Albana Metcalfe (1978), however, found no overall difference in self-concept between boys and girls during adolescence. Coleman's study (1974) also supported this view, emphasizing that self-concept remains similar between the sexes during this developmental stage.

Interestingly, women who reject traditional gender roles tend to display greater assertiveness and more positive self-concepts (Tolar, Kelly, & Stebbins, 1976). As gender roles evolve, women's behavior changes. Male counterparts are increasingly involved in housework, and the percentage of women in the labor force is rising (Green, 1985). Ahmed Shirdli, Kiswar, Sain, and Niti (1994) conducted a study using the Thematic Apperception Test (TAT) on Kinnauis Women of the Himalayas. They found that younger, educated, single women had the best self-image. Additionally, Markus Elliot (1990) noted that women's employment outside the home was associated with increased family income and ownership of family durables, which enhanced self-image among working women

Self-Concept and Occupational Choice

Different occupations have their own self-image, which reflects the characteristics required in those careers. Based on personality traits and needs, individuals are motivated to select particular occupations. Super et al. (1963) proposed a dominant theory in this regard, explaining that vocational adjustment depends on the implementation of self-concept, and an individual's self-concept determines their job choice. Reich and Geller (1976a, 1976b) found that various occupations have distinct self-images that mirror the necessary characteristics for those careers. Watkins (1976) also highlighted the influence of self-esteem on vocational choices. Chalungsooth and Porthip (1989) identified several factors (13 in total) that influence career decisions among females in South Asian culture. These factors include working conditions, family maintenance, work enjoyment, and job advantages.

Self-Concept and Women's Employment

Employment and vocational guidance are influenced by needs, requirements, and personality. According to Super et al. (1963), each person progresses through different life stages, each characterized by distinct vocational developmental tasks. The final choice of vocation reflects how thoroughly an individual has integrated their self-concept into the world of work. Putnam and Hansen (1972) conducted a study on female subjects and found that they tended to choose roles consistent with their self-concept. Davis (1969) and Reich and Geller (1976a) explored self-descriptions among female nurses, revealing that nurses aligned their characteristics with the requirements of their profession. Sinha (1973) indicated that personal characteristics—such as needs, attitudes, abilities, and self-concept—interfere with the smooth and almost automatic quality of interaction between individuals in job roles.

In a study by Gainor, Kathy, and Forrest Lind (1991), the complexity of career development issues among African American women was evident. Career choices positively influence self-concept. Reo Poteal, Mary, and Martin (1991) implemented a career awareness program for adolescent girls, resulting in increased confidence in choosing occupations and clearer ideas about potential career paths. Jenkins and Sharom Ral (1994) attributed affiliative values, power satisfaction, and improved self-concept to the structural power of women's occupational roles. Lenham and Janel Simonson (1990) found significantly higher self-esteem among professional women compared to homemakers and non-professional women. Furthermore, women's self-esteem was higher when their work status aligned with their initial role choice (whether as homemakers or professionals). The study also revealed that self-esteem increased when the rewards of marriage outweighed the concerns, and working women experienced higher self-esteem when work-related rewards prevailed. These findings underscore the critical relationship between an individual's sense of identity and self-esteem, particularly among women .

Self-Concept and Marital Adjustment

The development of self-concept is not static; it evolves under different conditions at various life stages. Marriage is a significant life event where spouses become essential to each other. The self-concept of an unmarried person may be redefined after marriage due to changing circumstances. Schumm, Walter, et al. (1980) studied the similarity in self-esteem as a function of the duration of marriage among student couples. They found that mate selection processes contribute to the observed similarity in self-esteem between husbands and wives. In the Indian context, Mandal and Gupta (1994) discovered that highly educated and high SES (socio-economic status) women held more liberal attitudes toward sex, marital status, and adjustment. Woods, Nancy, Lentz Martha, and Mitchell Ellen (1993) found that married women experiencing less stress were better educated, more adjusted, and had a better self-concept. Walker and Woods (1976) also reported that married women with higher masculinity and better self-concept received support from their husbands, leading to better overall adjustment.

Self-Concept and Sex Role

Self-concept is heavily influenced by sex roles. Biological sex identity is determined at birth, and later, children learn sex roles based on fixed societal norms and identification. The term "appropriate sex role behavior" refers to masculine or feminine behavior associated with male and female characteristics in our culture. However, this does not necessarily imply desirability. People exhibit either masculine or feminine attitudes, behaviors, and interests, but most individuals possess both characteristics (Bem, 1974, 1981, 1985; Helmreich, Spence & Wilhelm, 1981), a concept known as androgyny.

Stein, Sandra, and Weston Louise (1982) noted in their study that women who held more professional attitudes toward women's roles in contemporary society scored significantly higher on a measurement of identity achievement than women with more traditional attitudes. Nelson, Mary-Lee (1996) emphasized that girls' self-development relies on mutually empathic relationships with primary caretakers. Lafromboise, Teresa; Heyle, Anneliere; and Ozer, Emily (1990) found that the roles of Native American women developed as caretakers transmitted cultural influences, significantly impacting their self-concept.

Toda Kazuka and Katada Yayoi (1987) observed that familiar factors influenced the structure of sex role acceptance among female adolescents in Japan. Greenglass, Esther, and Devins Reva (1982) conducted a sex-role study and found that participants planned on having both a career and a family, but family remained their priority. Locksley and Calten (1979) discovered that women high in both masculinity and femininity were better adjusted than individuals who strictly adhered to sex-typed roles, both psychologically and sociologically. Cate, Rodney, Sugawara, Alan (1986), Orlofsky, Jacob, and Heron Connie (1987), Nezu, Asthur, Nezu Christine, Peterson, Marta (1986), and Paul Marilyn & Fisher Judith (1980) provided strong support for the masculinity model of self-esteem. Walker and Woods (1976) found that married women with more masculinity received support from their husbands, contributing to their overall well-being.

From Early Infancy: Gender Differences in Parental Perceptions

Parents tend to view their sons and daughters differently from early infancy. Newborn daughters are often described as smaller, softer, less attentive, cute, more delicate, and finer featured compared to their male counterparts. According to Krieger (1976) and Rubin, Provenzano, and Luria (1974), these differences in parental perceptions may play a crucial role in the sex typing process that influences self-concept. Sex differential treatment may limit girls' development of free exploration and promote greater conformity to cultural norms and values (Ruble, 1984).

Leung Wing-man Winnie (1994) found that students in single-sex schools had significantly higher self-concept scores than co-educational students. Interestingly, there was no interaction between school type and sex role type. In particular, androgynous individuals consistently scored highest in self-concept domains under study.

Sex Role

The Dance of Masculinity and Femininity: Breaking Stereotypes

Definition and Importance

In the early decades of the 20th century, Indian women primarily lived within the confines of their homes. Any work or contact outside these walls was considered against their dignity and honor. However, education has brought about significant changes. Women have become more conscious of their rights, and an increasing number of girls are attending schools and colleges. As female education grows and societal circumstances evolve, women are entering career fields.

Traditionally, women were associated with feminine qualities. Yet, the changing social landscape and women's career-oriented mindset have begun to impact the traditional sex roles of Indian women. They now seek the same considerations and opportunities that were previously reserved for men. Consequently, their traditional sex roles are shifting.

Biological sexual identity begins at birth, where infants are categorized as male or female. Masculine and feminine identities significantly influence behavior and self-concept. These roles refer to the constellation of characteristics and behaviors deemed appropriate and relevant within a society. Importantly, these roles are learned and culturally influenced, rather than innate.

The concept of being a masculine or feminine person extends beyond basic sexual functions. As Mussen (1961) explains, successful sex role identification is closely tied to effective personal social functioning.

An individual's perception of their own degree of masculinity or femininity is termed "sex role identity." This identity is a fundamental component of self-concept. Sex role typing is commonly known as masculine and feminine. Bem (1974) proposed that some people exhibit clear masculinity or femininity, while others develop both masculine and feminine characteristics, a state known as psychological androgyny.

The Role of Men and Women in the Social System

In the social fabric, the roles of men and women have been firmly established. These archetypal models of gender roles and status have existed since the earliest days of human society. Traditionally, men have been responsible for managing the external interface with the environment, while women have taken charge of the internal affairs within the home.

The Female Child's Emotive Map

As a female child grows, she constructs an emotive map of her family. Unfortunately, when parents display indifference toward her, she becomes aware that her status is secondary to that of her male counterparts. This realization can lead to doubts about her own self-worth. Consequently, her self-concept is affected, and she lacks clear anchors for her psychological identity—both within herself and within the larger societal framework. Researchers Tolor, Kelly, and Stebbins (1976) have found that the relationship between self-attitudes and acceptance of others tends to be stronger for women than for men.

Masculinity and Femininity

Sex role typing, commonly referred to as masculinity and femininity, begins early in life. Newborns are categorized as either male or female, and their behavior patterns are shaped by cultural and societal influences. Masculinity and femininity encompass a constellation of characteristics and behaviors that are considered appropriate and relevant for males and females during a specific era.

Androgyny: A Blend of Masculine and Feminine Traits

Contrary to the traditional binary view of masculinity and femininity, psychologist Sandra Bem (1974, 1975) introduced the concept of psychological androgyny. Dissatisfied with the notion that individuals had to fit neatly into one category or the other, Bem proposed that masculinity and femininity are orthogonal personality constructs. According to her, androgynous people possess both masculine and feminine qualities. They can assert their rights assertively in one moment and exhibit warmth and tenderness in the next. Bem (1981) argued that androgynous individuals are better equipped to adapt to various situations because they can draw from both sets of traits.

The Androgynous Person

The term "androgyny" combines "andro" (meaning "man") and "gyny" (meaning "woman"). An androgynous person embodies both traditional masculine qualities (such as independence, assertiveness, and competitiveness) and traditionally feminine traits (such as warmth, tenderness, and compassion). This blending of characteristics allows them to navigate life with flexibility and adaptability. These gender roles and concepts are not fixed; they evolve over time and vary across cultures. As we continue to explore human identity, it's essential to recognize the richness and diversity of individual experiences.

The Current Ideological Positions on Sex Roles of Women

Three distinct ideological positions shape our understanding of sex roles for women: Conservative, Moderate, and Radical. Let's delve into each of these perspectives:

Conservative Ideology: The "Housewife" Role: The conservative ideology places significant emphasis on the traditional "housewife" role for women. According to this view, a woman's primary purpose is to manage the household, and this role is expected to be a lifelong pursuit. The connection between women and domestic responsibilities is deeply entrenched within this perspective.

Moderate Ideology: Balancing Motherhood and Work: The moderate ideology seeks to strike a compromise between a woman's dual roles—as a mother and as a working professional. It acknowledges that women can contribute both within the family and in the workforce, aiming for a harmonious balance.

Radical Ideology: Absolute Gender Equality: The radical ideology advocates for complete equality between the sexes. It rejects the moderate position and calls for a fundamental shift in societal norms. Within this framework, work distribution between men and women should be equitable.

Emancipation and Rejecting Traditional Norms: True emancipation for women cannot be realized until they actively pursue lifelong careers and reject the idealized housewife role. Additionally, challenging the notion that family solely exists for their satisfaction is essential.

Ascribed vs. Achieved Roles

The distinction between ascribed and achieved roles is crucial. Sex roles fall into the category of ascribed roles—those assigned based on societal expectations. However, there often exists a conflict between these ascribed roles (such as femininity) and the practical requirements for effective performance.

Development of Sex Roles

Sex roles develop through identification. This largely unconscious process influences a growing child to think, feel, and behave similarly to significant figures in their life. Girls raised in environments emphasizing individual development tend to deviate more from conventional sex role standards than those from traditional backgrounds.

Influence of Parents and Environment

Parents serve as the original prototypes of masculinity and femininity for children. Later, the child's school environment and peer group contribute to shaping their sense of maleness or femaleness.

Physical Attributes and Self-Concept

During adolescence, physical attributes—such as height, weight, and body shape—play a crucial role in sex role identity. A positive body image contributes to a healthy self-conception. Our culture often assigns greater freedom, power, and value to the male role, which can lead girls to desire the more attractive male role. Unfortunately, this devaluation of the female role contributes to women viewing themselves as less adequate and more fearful than men. The development of sex roles is multifaceted, influenced by various factors.

Social Factors in Sex Role Development

The child learns to differentiate between the male and female role standards assigned by society. These distinctions are transmitted by parents and other agents of socialization. According to Kagan (1964), children identify with their same-sex parent because they perceive the power and resources held by that model. The child believes that by demonstrating sex-role-appropriate behavior, they too will acquire similar advantages. This process reinforces sex-typed self-concept traits, behaviors, and feelings.

Biological Factors

Biological factors play a significant role in sex role typing. Two areas of biological influence are particularly relevant:

Effects of Hormones on Sex Typing: Hormones are powerful chemical substances that interact with cells capable of receiving hormonal messages and responding to them. Androgens, such as testosterone, are male hormones, while estrogens and progesterones are female hormones. Researchers like Goy (1975), Hines (1982), and Hoyenga & Hoyenga (1979) highlight critical periods during prenatal development and puberty when the organism responds to hormones.

Hormones organize both psychological and biological predispositions toward masculinity or femininity during the prenatal period. The increase in hormones during puberty activates these early predispositions established during the organization phase.

Brain Localization and Sex Differences: The two hemispheres of the brain influence various behaviors. Researchers explore the relationship between sex differences in brain development and localization. While this area is complex, it underscores the interplay between biology and behavior.

Cognitive Factors

Children's own understanding of gender and sex roles significantly contributes to the developmental process. Kohlberg (1966) advocates for a cognitive approach to understanding sex-role development.

Self-Categorization Based on Physical and Sex Role Differences: Children categorize themselves as male or female based on observable differences, such as clothing, hairstyle, or occupation. Rubel (1984) notes that even at a very early age, children grasp sex-typed labels like "boy" and "girl" and apply them to activities, occupations, and playthings.

Sex Typing Before Gender Constancy: According to Fagot (1985), sex typing begins well before children have a stable concept of gender constancy (the understanding that gender remains consistent across situations). This sex role standard influences positive or negative self-evaluation of one's masculinity or femininity. The sex role development is multifaceted, influenced by both social and biological factors.

Cultural Factors

The culturally approved sex role identity stereotype functions as the ideal influencing factor to inspire individuals. Cultural reinforcements of the right behavior, selective presentation of toys, clothing, and hobbies influence sex role identities. Kagan (1964) reports that as early as 3 years old, boys are aware of some of the activities and objects that our culture regards as masculine.

Sex Role and Relevant Related Variables

Sex Role and Self-Concept

The global self-concept is attached to sex role typing. Sex role is a process whereby a growing child takes on the behavior and self-concept of another individual. A child's emerging self-concept is built on the foundation of their identification of sex role typing. It is a conscious process of copying specific behavior. From sex role identity, a major element of self-concept emerges. This sex role identity is a basic component of the self-concept.

In different studies, psychologists have given their views. According to Spence and Helmereich (1978), subjects scoring high feminine/low masculine display considerably lower self-esteem than those scoring high masculine/low feminine.

In most of the studies, adolescents' self-concepts find boys holding more positive self-concepts than girls. This lies in the fact that, in general, masculine attributes are more highly valued in Western society than the feminine ones (Sheriffs and Mc-Kee, 1957). Connell et al. (1975), Smith (1975), Bunrs (1977), and Broverman et al. (1972) believe that characteristics of sex role identity are still unchanged. Tolor and Stebbins (1976) have shown that women who reject their sex role stereotype display greater assertiveness and more positive self-concepts.

In another study, Fein et al. (1975) explained that girls who identify with both stereotypical feminine models and achievement models will experience role conflict and, hence, have lower self-esteem than boys. This is because the girls shift their source of self-esteem from achievement to heterosexual affiliation. Smith (1975), Cooper Smith (1967), and Cannell et al. (1975) confirmed the above investigation.

Wilson and Wilson (1976) explained that males and females have different sources for their self-esteem. Male self-esteem derives from success experiences in vocational positions of power and competition. Female self-esteem is derived from the achievement of personal goals, body image, existential concerns, and family relationships. More masculinity associated with high self-esteem is also found by Jones, Chernovetz, and Hansson (1978).

Sex Role and Family

Family plays a very important role in sex role development. From early infancy, parents are likely to view their sons and daughters differently. Various studies show that parents' perception of their male and female infants from the earlier days of life plays a role in the sex role typing process. Andersen Margaret (1991) reviewed the impact of feminist scholarship on family research by showing how the conceptualization of gender has transformed sociological understanding of the family. Gelfond Marjorie (1991) found that regarding the feminine sex role, females with less education suffer from agoraphobia (negative attitudes about traveling alone) compared to highly educated women. Toda Kazako and Katada Yayoi (1987) studied familial factors affecting the conscious structure of sex role acceptance in Japanese female adolescents.

Family roles and work roles are mutually reinforcing for women. Constraints in one realm structure roles in the other realm. This is especially true for normative expectations and behavior during early childhood and family formation. Many studies indicate that the causal relationship between nonfamilial experience and sex role orientation is conditional. Analysis of unmarried women in the first few years after high school indicates that neither college attendance nor occupational training alters sex role orientation (Huber and Spitze, 1981).

Sex Role and Education

Education also plays an important role in the determination of sex role type. In this regard, various studies show how education has influenced sex role types.

In a Swedish study, Gustafson, Sigrid, Staltin, Haka, and Magnusson David (1989) pointed out that education-oriented achievement motivation is a significantly valid indicator of sex role orientation.

In another study related to feminine sex roles, Gelfond Marjorie (1991) found that females with less education suffer from negative attitudes about traveling alone compared to highly educated women. Lafromboise, Teresa, Heyle, Anneliere, and Ozer Emily (1990) found in their study that sex roles of Native Americans prior to European contact were effective means of overcoming problems and achieving self-determination, particularly related to education.

Sex Role and Aspiration

Various studies have shown that there is a relationship between aspiration and sex role type. Horner (1972) postulated that women anticipate social rejection for succeeding in sex-typical careers. This phenomenon is interpreted as a motive to avoid success and a factor contributing to sex-typed aspirations. Although subsequent research has not consistently confirmed sex differences in fear of success (Levine & Crumrine, 1975), the concept cannot be unequivocally rejected. Many studies show an association between individual sex-role orientations and women's aspirations (Lipman-Blumen, 1972). Cornack (1961) writes that the basic factor in feminine power and the fulfillment of womanhood is the differentiation of sex and function without competition.

Sex Role & Employment

Employment and its nature affect sex role. The roles of men and women are fixed in the social system, but they are changing with the evolving scenario and career-orientedness of today's women. Certainly, this change has affected traditional sex roles. It is taking place for better adjustment to the prevailing situation. Employment in women and family responsibility constrain women's lives, but it also enhances confidence and helps develop certain qualities. As Mussen (1961) explained, masculinity/femininity determines global adjustment. Various studies also show that employment is associated with sex role. Locksley and Calten (1979) found that women intending to pursue careers and better adjust to both career and households exhibit androgynous traits. However, Burns et al. (1977) explain that characteristics of sex-role identity remain unchanged in employed women (Boverman et al.). Similarly, Putnam and Hansen (1972) found that female subjects choose employment based on feminine role concepts.

Sex Role & Marriage

Marriage and marital adjustment are also influenced by sex role. Sex role is a learned process, and the ideal picture of Indian feminine women is that of an adjustable and homely housewife. Women who identify themselves as ideal feminine women will try to display and adjust better in their family and marital life. As Cormack (1961) explained, the basic factor in feminine power and the fulfillment of sex and function is without competition. Similarly, Indira (1955) expressed her view that "Women spend the whole day considering matters entirely related to the house and particularly attending to the needs and desires of their lord—always subordinating their own comforts and convenience to their husband." In a recent study, Gottman (1994) found that in most marriages, wives are the ones who try to maintain the relationship. Mandal and Gupta (1994) reported that educated women had more liberal attitudes toward women, sex, and marital status. Their marital harmony also affects their sex role and attitudes.

Marital Adjustment

Thriving Through Marital Changes: Balancing Marital Roles

Definition and Importance

The traditional concept of marriage and marital adjustment in India is considered a sacrament, joining together two human beings into an eternal and indissoluble union. Marriage is viewed as a social duty toward the family and the community, rather than primarily for individual gratification or personal interests. In the early decades of the century, as Kapadia (1958) expressed, "marriage was considered a social duty towards the family and the community, with little emphasis on individual interests." The social background provided by authoritarian joint families and caste systems, dominating all spheres of life, left little room for recognizing personal factors or individual aspirations in the relationship between husband and wife. Ross (1961) explains how relatively good marital adjustment was possible within the framework of traditional Indian families. The large joint family provided contemporaries of similar age and sex, allowing companionship satisfaction without complete dependence on each other for deep affection or companionship. This facilitated marital adjustment in traditional Indian families, where roles were complementary. A wife's role was more definite, with specific duties, adhering to established patterns of conduct. Indira (1955) expressed similar views, highlighting how women spent their days attending to household matters and their husband's needs, subordinating their own comforts and convenience.

In the transition period, the definition of marital adjustment depends on the prevailing conception of marriage and societal standards. Locke and Williamson (1958) define marital adjustment as "the presence of characteristics in a marriage that tend to avoid or resolve conflicts, create satisfaction with the marriage and each other, share common interests and activities, and fulfill marital expectations." They further explain that marital adjustment involves companionship, agreement on basic values, affectional intimacy, accommodation, euphoria, and other unidentified factors. Ruch (1970) describes marital success as partly dependent on finding the right partner and partly on being the right partner. However, simply being suited to each other does not guarantee a successful marriage; couples must learn to live together, accommodating, compromising, and planning together.

In a recent study, Gottman (1994) challenges the stereotype of a happy marriage as one where couples like each other, understand each other well, and settle disputes easily. Stable marriages may not always fit this stereotype—some are volatile, with passionate fights and reconciliations, while others carefully avoid conflicts by agreeing to disagree.

Broadly speaking, marital adjustment refers to the state of the relationship in marriage where both husband and wife experience overall happiness and satisfaction with their marriage and each other.

Marital Adjustment in the Context of Western Culture

When comparing Indian and Western marriages, we find stark differences not only in how the marriage bond is established but also in the overall attitude toward marriage. In Indian society, marriages are predominantly arranged by families or elder members, whereas in Western culture, couples have more autonomy in decision-making. This difference can significantly impact marital adjustment. David Olson (1995-2000), a researcher from the University of Minnesota who studied over 15,000 married couples, recently asserted that approximately 50% of married individuals will never be truly happy unless they receive exceptional therapy.

Other researchers, such as Stern (1985), suggest that around 30% of marriages are "empty shells" characterized by minimal love, communication, and joy. Only about 25% of couples experience genuinely fulfilling marriages. The remaining 25% could potentially achieve a good marriage through therapy or by actively developing necessary skills through training or marriage enrichment programs.

A study conducted by Hanny Lighfoot-Klen (1989) on Sudanese females sheds light on marital adjustment. In Sudan, marriages are arranged by families, although some flexibility exists among the more modern and educated class. During marriage ceremonies, both the bride and groom adhere to rigidly assigned roles. Women's societal roles emphasize submission to their husbands, extreme modesty, unwavering chastity, and withdrawal from the external world.

Marital Adjustment in the Context of Indian Culture

In Indian culture, the concept of marriage places responsibility on the individuals themselves to create harmonious situations. Rather than viewing adjustment as a problem, Indian couples recognize the need to adapt to each other's tastes, temperaments, and preferences. They prioritize compromise over separation.

Prabhu (1958) refers to Manu's "Manusmriti," emphasizing that once united through the nuptial ceremony, couples should always strive to avoid conflict and remain faithful to each other. Radha Krishnan (1956) further observes, "We do not marry the women we love, but we love the women we marry."

Ross (1961) suggests that good marital adjustment is achievable within the framework of traditional Indian families. Dube (1955) and Srinivas (1942) argue that traditional norms in Indian society minimize conflicts related to adjustment, often resolved through cultural values and rationalization. Moorthy (1954) highlights binding elements in husband-wife relationships, emphasizing the need for adjustments consistent with dignity, personality, and destiny.

A recent study by Mandal and Gupta (1994) found that educated women exhibit more liberal attitudes toward women, sex, and marital status. Their marital harmony significantly influences their overall attitudes.

Marital Adjustment and Common Problems

After marriage, adjustment can be categorized into different groups: very good, average, poor, and very poor. Weiten (1986) has identified common problems related to marital adjustment.

Poor Communication

Recent studies emphasize the crucial role of communication in marital adjustment. Communication encompasses every message, feeling, desire, and thought conveyed to one's partner. While some forms of communication enhance marital adjustment, others can be destructive. Notably, poor communication ranks as the most common complaint (68%) among couples seeking counseling. Researchers such as Brehm (1985), Derlega (1984), and Gottman (1979, 1994) have extensively studied communication problems in the context of marital adjustment.

Financial Issue or Money Problems

Conflicts often arise due to financial issues, which can also impact dual-career couples. Sometimes both partners seek independent income, either out of necessity or due to an improved economic status. Kurdek (1993) has highlighted that low income can lead to marital discord.

Role Expectations

Partners may hold vastly different role expectations, including divisions of household chores, child-rearing responsibilities, cooking, and work outside the home. Traditionally, societal norms dictated specific roles for husbands and wives. However, education, awareness, and the rise of dual-career couples have led to changing dynamics. Some conflicts in marital adjustment stem from these evolving role expectations and the shifting status of women.

Contrary to popular belief, research indicates that a wife working outside the home does not necessarily increase marital problems or negatively impact children's development. In a study titled "The Relationship Between Marital Satisfaction, Division of Housework, and Child Care Tasks Among Dual-Career Couples," Durkace (Judith Anne, 1987) found no significant relationship between the division of household labor and overall marital satisfaction. Interestingly, wives tended to perform more family-related tasks than their husbands.

Emotional Responsiveness of Men and Women

In examining the emotional dynamics within marriages, Gottman (1994) discovered that, in most cases, wives take on the primary role of maintaining the relationship. However, when wives become unhappy, they tend to express their emotions through complaints and emotional reactions. In contrast, men often avoid negative emotions and instead focus on rational problem-solving. Unfortunately, this difference in emotional responsiveness can lead to "emotional overload" and contribute to marital adjustment issues. Women generally exhibit greater social sensitivity than men. They excel in active listening, empathy, and providing comforting responses (Brehm, Powel & Coke, 1989).

On the downside, Tannen (1990) observed that women tend to display stronger negative emotions during conflicts. Another study by Raus, Barry, Hertel & Swain (1974) suggests that married men engage in more effective communication with their wives. This includes showing concern for their wives' feelings, offering reassurance, seeking forgiveness, suggesting compromises, and maintaining a calm, problem-oriented approach during arguments (Rush, Barry, Hertel & Swain, 1974). White (1989) also found that both men and women contribute to marital troubles when they are dissatisfied.

Marital Adjustment and Relevant Variables

The advent of technology and societal changes have compelled women to adapt their interpersonal behavior to new environments. Consequently, traditional roles and status definitions have shifted. These transformations impact the concept of work, the nature of roles, and the meaning of women's roles in society. With each transition, women face changing horizons, role definitions, and societal values. These shifts also influence marital adjustment among Indian women. Relevant factors related to marital adjustment can be categorized into two groups: objective and subjective factors.

Marital Adjustment and Age

The age of both spouses at the time of marriage, their current ages, and the age difference between husband and wife can significantly affect marital adjustment. Several studies have explored this relationship. For instance, Terman (1938) found no consistent correlation between happiness and the age of either spouse at marriage. Burgess (1948, 1950) and Cotterll (1933) confirmed that moderate correlation exists between marital adjustment and the fact that both partners are between 22 and 30 years old at the time of marriage. From a psychological perspective, Prabhu (1958), Hart and Shields (1926), and Popenoe (1935) suggest that individuals should marry after reaching physical, emotional, and intellectual maturity.

Marital Adjustment and Age Difference in Husband and Wife

In Indian culture, a majority of women, whether employed or unemployed, marry men who are senior to them in age. It is commonly believed that this age difference contributes to harmony and happiness in marital relationships.

According to Bernard (1938), women reported the highest satisfaction with their husbands when the husbands were 0 to 5 years older than they were. Men, on the other hand, tended to be most satisfied with wives who were 0 to 10 years younger than themselves. However, research by Mckinney (1949), Terman (1938), Mowrer (1928), and Landies & Landies (1958) suggests that age differences between couples are not highly significant factors affecting overall happiness. There is no conclusive evidence that the husband must be older than the wife for effective marital adjustment. Interestingly, Smith (1969) found that age differentials have little impact on reported happiness among couples. Terman et al. (1938) even discovered that in cases where wives were considerably older than their husbands, those couples reported the highest levels of happiness.

Marital Adjustment and Level of Education of Husband and Wife

Over the last few decades, the educational qualifications of women have significantly increased. Consequently, the impact of educational levels on marital adjustment has become an important area of study. Various researchers have explored this relationship and provided differing views:

Kapoor (1970) found no definitive relationship between marital adjustment and the educational level of employed or unemployed women, nor with the educational level of the husband.

Chesser (1956) similarly reported that there was almost no association between the difference in educational levels of husbands and wives.

Folsom (1948), however, pointed out that Terman's findings suggested a moderate superiority of higher-educated women in terms of marital happiness.

Roth and Peck (1951) presented a different perspective. Referring to Terman's study, they noted that wives who were markedly superior to their husbands in education had lower happiness scores, while scores were higher when husbands were markedly superior in education.

Marital Adjustment and Number of Children

The arrival of a new baby in the family increases the responsibilities of the mother. She must devote more time and attention to the children, especially if she is also working. Balancing work and childcare can lead to tension, potentially affecting marital adjustment. Increased irritations and strains may make it challenging for her to maintain marital harmony and happiness.

Regarding the association between working women's marital adjustment and the number of their children, Nye and Hoffman (1963) found almost no relationship. The number of children did not significantly impact marital adjustment. Terman and Buttenwierer (1935) also reported no correlation between the number of children and marital happiness.

Marital Adjustment and Family Structure

The type and structure of a family can significantly impact the lifestyle of women. Whether a family is nuclear or joint has its own advantages and drawbacks. According to Kapoor (1970), the family type in which an employed or unemployed woman lives may influence her marital and family relationships, ultimately affecting her family adjustment. The composition of the family she resides in is closely related to her adjustment in married life. Kapoor's study revealed a fair degree of association between male marital adjustment and family composition. Upon comparison, nuclear families had the highest proportion of well-adjusted marriages. In maladjusted groups, the number of women living in joint families was three times higher than those living in nuclear families.

Marital Adjustment and Income Levels of Husband and Wife

The income disparity between husbands and employed wives can lead to maladjustment. Researchers have explored the relationship between the income levels of husbands and wives and their marital adjustment. Kapoor (1970) found that approximately 82% of husbands earned more than their wives, while 18% of women earned as much as or more than their husbands. There is a small association between a wife's marital adjustment and the income difference between husband and wife. Interestingly, husbands who earn less than their wives tend to be part of maladjusted marital groups.

Marital Adjustment and Occupational Status of Husband and Wife

Among employed women, their marital life can be influenced by both their own occupation and their husband's occupation. Different occupations have varying working hours and priorities, impacting the lives of employed women. Nye (1963) compared employed and unemployed women within four occupational groups based on their husbands' occupations to explore the relationship between the husband's employment status and marital adjustment. However, none of the analyses revealed significant differences.

Nye and Hoffman (1963) further explained the status of employed women and marital adjustment. Employment itself is relatively satisfying for well-educated women working in professional and high-status occupations. Employment enhances self-respect and fosters relatively satisfying interpersonal relationships. However, this feeling, directly or indirectly associated with employment, may negatively affect marital adjustment in lower socio-economic families.

Chesser (1956) found different results. English women showed a more definite association between their feelings about marital happiness and their own occupations than between marital happiness and their husband's occupation.

Marital Adjustment and Reasons for Taking Up a Job

The changing landscape of education, industrialization, and urbanization has significantly influenced the attitudes of young, educated Indian women. Personal needs, such as recognition, emotional fulfillment, security, and socioeconomic status (SES), have driven many women to pursue employment. This new role of women in the workforce has also impacted their marital lives and overall adjustment.

Research by Dobbs, Moneck, Graham, and Richard (1994) indicates that education and high qualifications positively influence self-concept, which in turn affects marital adjustment. Similarly, Gainor Kathy and Forrest Lind (1991) found that educated working women tend to have a high self-concept, leading to better marital adjustment. Mandal and Gupta (1994) also reported that highly educated women exhibit a more positive attitude toward marital adjustment.

Marital Adjustment and Satisfaction with Job

It is commonly assumed that if an employed woman is satisfied with her job, she is better positioned to make adjustments in her marriage. Conversely, dissatisfaction with her job can adversely affect marital harmony.

A study by Jenkins and Ral (1994) explored the "structural power of women's occupational roles." They found that women in relational power jobs reported affiliative values and interpersonal power satisfaction, contributing to a positive self-concept and influencing marital adjustment. Research by Nye and Hoffman (1963) supports the idea that wives' employment can increase marital conflict.

Marital Adjustment and Sharing Household Tasks

Agreement between husband and wife on sharing household responsibilities appears to impact marital adjustment. Kapoor (1970) observed that extremely well-adjusted marriages were more common among couples who consistently agreed on sharing household tasks.

However, Durkac and Judith (1987) conducted a study on "The Relationship Between Marital Satisfaction and Division of Housework and Childcare Tasks Among Dual-Career Couples" and found no significant relationship between housework division and marital satisfaction.

Marital Adjustment and Complaints Between Spouses

Women tend to express more complaints about their spouses and marriages compared to men (Brehm, 1985). Tannen (1990) noted that women exhibit stronger negative emotions during conflicts. In general, during milder disagreements, the sexes often find themselves at odds. Women seek emotional responses and want emotional validation, while men provide more informal, unemotional responses and prefer practical, constructive, and rational feedback. Poor communication, characterized by a steady flow of criticism or blame, can lead to maladjustment in marriage. However, if both sexes learn to provide both emotional and practical responses, it can improve understanding and strengthen relationships between partners (Tannen, 1990; Gray, 1993).

Marital Adjustment and Status of Husband and Wife

Agreement between husband and wife regarding each other's status significantly influences marital adjustment. When both partners agree on their relative positions—whether inferior, superior, or equal—it tends to facilitate smoother adjustment in married life.

Kapoor (1970) demonstrated in her research that among working women, those who consistently agreed with their husbands about their respective family statuses had an impressive 98% rate of extremely well-adjusted marriages. Conversely, among those who consistently disagreed on this point, 97% experienced maladjustment or extreme maladjustment.

Husband-Wife Agreement on Wife's Employment and Marital Adjustment

Among working women, some take up jobs primarily because their husbands encourage them to work. It is generally assumed that agreement between the working woman and her husband regarding her employment status positively affects marital adjustment. Conversely, disagreement on this issue can adversely impact marital adjustment. Kapoor (1970) reported in her study that 70% of husbands of working women wanted their wives to work.

Sex Roles and Marital Adjustment

Traditionally, Indian marriage was not primarily about individual gratification or personal aspirations; it was a social duty. The roles of husband and wife were complementary. According to societal norms, the husband was expected to be the authoritative figure, with his will dominating the domestic scene. The wife was to regard him as her master and serve him faithfully, occupying a subordinate role (Dube, 1955).

However, the changing landscape—driven by education and employment opportunities—has altered sex roles for women, affecting marital adjustment. It is believed that working women exhibit more masculine traits than non-working women. Consequently, the marital adjustment of working women with these masculine traits may be influenced. Numerous studies have explored this topic, yielding diverse views and results.

Feinauer, Leslie L., and Williams Evans, Linda (1989), studied dual-career couples and found that marital adjustment was influenced only when the husband did not consent to the wife's employment. The study revealed that women forced into jobs and possessing feminine traits experienced poor marital adjustment.

In an Indian study, Srivastava (1989) discovered a significant relationship between sex role conception, ego development, and marital harmony. Marital harmony was negatively related to conscious ego levels and positively related to androgynous sex role conception. These results suggest that marital adjustment depends on the integration of both high masculinity and high femininity. Interestingly, the research by Durka, Judith, and Anne (1987) found no significant relationship between housework division (role division) and marital adjustment.

Haveman and West (1952) found that employed women have a higher rate of divorce than non-employed ones because employed women have to play both roles. In another study, Nye (1959) found that where women were employed, marital adjustment scores more frequently showed unhappiness and dissatisfaction. However, Bowman (1954) presented a different result: wife's employment can lead to a closer relationship between husband and wife because sometimes the husband supports the wife's masculine role, resulting in harmony in marriage.

According to Jephcott, Seear, and Smith (1962), the partnership between husband and wife was thought to be growing closer, and some people believed that married women's employment, far from threatening good relations, actually helped to improve them. Similarly, Ross (1961) demonstrated that marriage can be strengthened and enriched by a wife's return to study and work, where she could also play a masculine role. On the other hand, Locke and Mackeprang (1949) found "no significant difference" between the marital adjustment of working and non-working women. Acharya (1998) highlighted the challenges of managing societal conditions while doing justice to both roles as a wife and a working woman.

Higher Education and Marital Adjustment

Educated women achieve and maintain harmony and happiness in their married and family life, even with the added role of working women. A study by Lenham, Janel, and Simonson (1990) revealed that educated working women have high self-esteem, and the rewards outweigh concerns about marriage. Additionally, Mandal and Gupta (1994) found that women with higher education and socioeconomic status had more liberal attitudes toward women's sex and marital status, with marital harmony significantly affecting these attitudes.

Present Study

Need of the Study

The present study aims to investigate the relationship between self-concept, sex-role, and marital adjustment among employed and unemployed educated married women.

Review of previous studies and literature surveys has shown that most research on women has focused either on their current status or their experiences throughout their lives. In recent times, there have been studies on educated women or women in the workforce, but many of these studies provide a vivid picture of educated women and their interpersonal relations within the family. In some other studies where psychological variables have been examined, there is scant reference to women, especially those who are part of the working force. Therefore, the investigator felt the need to study several psychological variables of both working and non-working educated women to ascertain a clear process of influence on personality variables from the workplace to the family.

Rapid changes are taking place in society. Recently acquired legal and political rights, education, awareness of women's rights, and gender equality have transformed the attitudes of educated women. Work now holds deep meaning in women's lives. They are breaking through the hard shell of traditionalism to fulfill their various psychological and personal needs. Observations by the investigator have shown that many educated women are taking up various jobs due to various reasons. This led the investigator to explore the changes occurring among these educated working women in relation to their self-concept, sex-role, and marital adjustment.

Self-Concept

Self-concept plays a crucial role in understanding behavior. It is related to energizing, directing, and sustaining psycho-social behavior. Various feedback and sources significantly contribute to the development of self-concept. Through this study, the investigator aims to understand the extent of self-concept among working and non-working women separately. This analysis will be based on social comparison, feedback, and appraisal.

Sex-Role Differentiation

Many studies have addressed sex-role differentiation among males and females. Sex roles serve as fundamental mechanisms for channeling and integrating work and family roles. In this context, there is a need to investigate the psychological masculinity and femininity of educated employed and unemployed married women. Shedding light on the psychological strategies utilized by these women in coping with the various demands of their day-to-day lives is essential.

Marital Adjustment

The investigator also aims to determine how successfully educated married employed and unemployed women achieve and maintain harmony and happiness in their married lives. By assessing the extent of marital adjustment among these women, the study will uncover the changes imposed by the added role on the marital patterns of educated employed married women.

Marriage: An Exploration of Self-Concept, Sex Roles, and Marital Adjustment

Introduction

Marriage holds immense significance in an individual's life. However, the changing social landscape and the increasing career orientation of women have begun to impact traditional gender roles in Indian society. Women now aspire to the same considerations and opportunities that were previously reserved for men. Consequently, their traditional roles are evolving. In light of these developments, the investigator seeks to understand the interplay between personality traits—specifically self-concept, sex roles, and marital adjustment—among today's educated women. Additionally, the study aims to explore how these variables interact with each other.

Study Objectives

Influence of Employment Status on Women's Personality: The study aims to delineate the influence of employment status (employed vs. unemployed) on the personality makeup of contemporary women. To achieve this, several psychological variables—self-concept, sex roles, and marital adjustment—have been selected for investigation. This exploratory, inductive study aligns with the qualitative research agenda in the work-family-personality domain.

Understanding Self-Concept: Self-concept comprises various factors, which can be theoretically divided into three components: conceptual, perceptual, and attitudinal. The study seeks to determine the magnitude of these components separately among both the study group (employed women) and the comparison group (unemployed women). By analyzing these differences at a micro level, we can gain insights into self-concept variations.

Exploring Changing Sex Roles: The study investigates the different types of sex roles within both groups. By examining sex-role concepts in the present context, we can ascertain how societal perceptions are evolving.

Marital Adjustment Strength and Magnitude: Assessing the strength and magnitude of marital adjustment among employed and unemployed women individually and collectively is crucial. This allows us to understand the impact of work on marital adjustment and explore how educated women navigate their marital lives.

Testing Relationships: The study tests the relationships between self-concept, sex roles, and marital adjustment. By understanding these interconnections, we can uncover how these variables influence each other.

Complementary Variables: The variables in this study are complementary. We assume that psychosocial conditions play a role in determining their magnitude and direction. Therefore, we aim to explore the complementary nature of these variables and their influence on each other.

Reciprocal Relationships: Finally, the study examines the reciprocal relationship between the variables. By doing so, we can better understand how they interact and influence one another.

Hypotheses

On the basis of a few studies, day-to-day observations, and literature survey, the following hypotheses were formulated:

* Self-concept of employed women will differ significantly from that of unemployed women.

* The perceptual, conceptual, and attitudinal components of self-concept will differ significantly among employed and unemployed women groups.

* High scorers of self-concept will be more in the employed women group than in the unemployed women group, whereas low scorers of self-concept will be less in the employed women group than in the unemployed women group.

* There will be a significant difference in sex-role type among employed and unemployed women groups.

* There will be more androgynous/masculine sex-role type women in the employed group than in the unemployed women group.

* Composition of employed and unemployed women groups in respect of sex-role type (Feminine - Female, Masculine Female, and absolute androgyny) will differ significantly.

* Marital adjustment of employed and unemployed women groups will differ significantly.

* Self-concept will be related with sex-role type in both employed and unemployed women groups.

* Self-concept will be related with marital adjustment in both employed and unemployed women groups.

* Sex-role type and marital adjustment will be related in both employed and unemployed women groups.

* Women of high self-concept will have masculine/androgynous sex-role type, whereas low self-concept women will have feminine sex-role type and vice versa.

* Women having high level of self-concept will have good marital adjustment than women having low level of self-concept and vice versa.

* Women having masculine/androgynous sex-role type will have good marital adjustment than women having feminine sex-role type and vice versa.

* Employed women having masculine/androgynous sex-role type will have high self-concept than the unemployed women having feminine sex-role type.

* Employed women having high marital adjustment will have high self-concept than the unemployed women having low marital adjustment.

* Employed women having high self-concept will have masculine/androgynous sex-role type, whereas unemployed women having low self-concept will have feminine sex-role type.

* Employed women having high marital adjustment will have masculine/androgynous sex-role type, whereas unemployed women having low marital adjustment will have feminine sex-role type.

* Employed women having high self-concept will have high marital adjustment than the unemployed women having low self-concept.

* Employed women having masculine/androgynous sex-role type will have high marital adjustment than the unemployed women having feminine sex-role type.

* Women having masculine/androgynous sex-role type and high marital adjustment will have high self-concept than the women having feminine sex-role type and low level of marital adjustment.

* Women having high self-concept and high marital adjustment will have masculine/androgynous sex-role type, whereas women having low self-concept and low marital adjustment will have feminine sex-role type.

* Women having high self-concept and masculine/androgynous sex-role type will have high marital adjustment than the women having low self-concept and feminine sex-role type.

* Level of self-concept, type of sex-role, and level of marital adjustment will depend upon interaction between the variables as well as status.

Salient Feature

* Many research findings demonstrate the effect of women's employment on family life and the impact of family life on work behavior. However, less attention has been given to the conscious experience of women. The present study focuses on the psycho-social behavior of women. Investigating these variables will shed light on the psychological

experiences and psycho-social makeup of today's Indian women. Thus, the study aims to explore the unique combination of family, work, and personality among today's women to better understand their individuality.

* This exploratory research examines the interdependence of work and family roles for women, which has direct relevance for economic, political, and social policies, as well as job design characteristics. It also addresses the specific interests of women in these roles.

* To enhance the scientific rigor of the study, the investigator also examined a comparative group of unemployed women. This additional group provides valuable insights into the psychological variables under study.

* The study's variables were measured using valid and reliable psychological tests and checklists suitable for the Indian context.

* The two groups of women selected for this study come from the urban population of Dhanbad. Analyzing these women within a well-defined and homogeneous group will yield greater insights into the research problem.

* Unlike much of the earlier work that focused on a narrow range of occupations, this study covers a broad spectrum of occupations.

* Lastly, the investigator diligently collected data from a large number of employed and unemployed women, considering various demographic variables. This approach ensures scientific rigor in the methodology.

CHAPTER II Methodology: Quantifying the Unseen

Sample

The present field study is designed to test hypotheses related to the family-work domain and personality dynamics of women. For testing the hypotheses of the present study, two groups of women were randomly selected from the urban population: (1) educated employed women and (2) educated unemployed women.

The group of educated employed women was composed of a diverse sample from different types of organizations and mixed occupation groups. It included teachers from middle and high schools, lecturers and professors from colleges, scientists, and office staff from research institutes, as well as officers and office staff from non-government and government offices (e.g., CMPDI, BCCL, CMRI & CFRI). Additionally, doctors and self-employed professionals (such as beauticians and fashion designers) were part of this group.

The group of educated unemployed women was also composed of a diverse sample, similar to the educated employed women group. It included unemployed housewives whose husbands were working in the same type of organizations and occupations, and at the same capacity, from where the educated employed women group was selected.

To ensure the inclusion of relevant respondents, several restrictions were imposed. Only those participants who were educated up to at least the graduation level, married, had a minimum of four years of marital life, fell within the age range of 25 to 50 years, belonged to different categories of the number of children (four categories - see Table 2.5), and came from different types of family structures (two categories - see Table 2.4) were considered. Additionally, participants were required to have a minimum of 4 years of tenure in their occupation. As a result, the sample characteristics of both groups were kept similar in terms of education, marital status, length of marital life, age range, number of children, family structure, and tenure in the occupation. The process of random sampling involved selecting a comparison group based on the relevance of the study. Literature suggests that individuals may differ in self-concept, sex-role, and marital adjustment based on factors such as age, parental status, occupation type, education level, income, length of marital life, and number of children. Careful consideration was given to selecting a sample with adequate variation along these dimensions, despite the constraints in sample selection.

Procedure

An initial pool of potential samples from both groups was identified using various sources outlined previously. The semi-structured interview began with demographic questions about the respondents' personal backgrounds, occupations, work histories, family structures, ages, lengths of marital life, and number of children. This information provided data to categorize the respondents based on personal characteristics as well as work and family life. The required sample was then contacted and convinced to participate in the study. Sixty-seven percent of the contacted housewives and eighty-two percent of employed women agreed to participate. They were given a questionnaire, including a personal data sheet, to be completed privately. The return rate was higher among unemployed women (94%) than the employed women group (81%). Working women volunteered to complete the questionnaire after normal working hours.

All participants were instructed to complete the questionnaire, and data were collected in person. The investigator also asked subjects about any difficulties they encountered while answering the questionnaires. If participants did not return the questionnaires within a scheduled period, a follow-up reminder was given. Some participants refused to take up the questionnaire again, resulting in missing data. The sample size was reduced to 213 in the non-working group and 208 in the working group.

All participants in the study were voluntary, and questionnaires were identified by code numbers only. Prior to their participation, subjects were assured of complete confidentiality regarding their questionnaire responses. They were informed that only aggregate data (not personal information) would be reported. Participants had the option not to mention their names in the personal data sheet.

The research topic generated interest among women themselves, and they cooperated willingly. However, data collection from housewives was difficult and time-consuming.

At the beginning of the study, it was unclear how candid women would be about their personality dynamics or how open they would be about their marital lives. During and after the data collection process, if requested information was unobtainable or found to be false, the case was omitted from the sample.

Data collection began after the summer vacation in July 1996 and continued through February 1997. Among the total responses, only 96% contained complete data sets suitable for testing the proposed hypotheses. For the analysis of the present study, data from both groups were randomly reduced to an equal number. The methods for organizing and reducing qualitative data have been discussed by several researchers, including Glaser and Straus (1967), Piotrkowski (1979), and Wiseman (1947). Therefore, a total of 400 subjects—200 in the unemployed women group and 200 in the employed women group—were considered for the present study.

Self-Concept Scale

The self-concept scale was developed by Rastogi (1979) and standardized on Indian adults. It addresses three aspects of self-concept: Perceptual, Conceptual, and Attitudinal components. According to Hurlock (1974), self-concept comprises three major components. The scale includes ten constructs distributed across these three components:

Perceptual Component

This component focuses on "Health and Sex Appropriateness." It resembles the physical self-concept, considering factors such as appearance, attractiveness, sex appropriateness of the body, and the importance of different body parts. Six items in the scale measure the perceptual component.

Conceptual Component

The conceptual component encompasses constructs related to ability, sociability, and emotional maturity. It aligns with the psychological self-concept, which involves an individual's origin, abilities, disabilities, social adjustment, and personality traits. Sixteen items in the scale measure the conceptual component.

Attitudinal Components

This component includes constructs related to self-acceptance, worthiness, beliefs about the present, past, and future, as well as feelings of shame and guilt. Attitudinal components reflect a person's attitudes toward their current status, future prospects, self-esteem, pride, shame, beliefs, convictions, and values. Twenty-nine items in the scale measure the attitudinal component of self-concept.

The scale is self-administered and employs a five-point response scale. Respondents indicate their agreement with each statement using the following options: Strongly Agree, Agree, Undecided, Disagree, or Strongly Disagree. There is no time limit, but all items should be responded to within 30 minutes. The scale includes both positive and negative items. Positive items are scored from five (Strongly Agree) to one (Strongly Disagree), while negative items are scored in reverse. The mean score for the constructs and the entire scale is 173 for females.

Additionally, the scale provides separate mean values for the three major components of self-concept: Perceptual, conceptual, and attitudinal.

I. Self-Concept Scale

The self-concept scale was developed by Rastogi (1979) and standardized on Indian adults. It addresses three aspects of self-concept: Perceptual, Conceptual, and Attitudinal components. According to Hurlock (1974), self-concept comprises three major components. The scale includes ten constructs distributed across these three components:

Perceptual Component

This component focuses on "Health and Sex Appropriateness." It resembles the physical self-concept, considering factors such as appearance, attractiveness, sex appropriateness of the body, and the importance of different body parts. Six items in the scale measure the perceptual component, with a mean value of 19 for females.

Conceptual Component

The conceptual component encompasses constructs related to ability, sociability, and emotional maturity. It aligns with the psychological self-concept, which involves an individual's origin, abilities, disabilities, social adjustment, and personality traits. Sixteen items in the scale measure the conceptual component, with a mean value of 52 for females.

Attitudinal Components

This component includes constructs related to self-acceptance, worthiness, beliefs about the present, past, and future, as well as feelings of shame and guilt. Attitudinal components reflect a person's attitudes toward their current status, future prospects, self-esteem, pride, shame, beliefs, convictions, and values. Twenty-nine items in the scale measure the attitudinal component of self-concept, with a mean value of 102 for females.

Reliability and Validity

The scale demonstrates reliability and validity. Using the split-half method with Spearman-Brown prophecy formula, the reliability coefficient was found to be 0.87.

Content validity was determined using Thurstone's method of equal appearing intervals (Edwards, 1969). Discriminability of each item and item homogeneity were statistically assessed.

II. Masculinity - Femininity Check List

The masculinity-femininity checklist, developed by Sinha (1986), is a standardized test containing 40 adjectives related to masculinity and femininity (20 each). These adjectives were derived from Indian samples of males and females (see Appendix II).

Scoring

The checklist categorizes adjectives into four groups:

PM (Positive Masculinity)

NM (Negative Masculinity)

PF (Positive Femininity)

NF (Negative Femininity)

Respondents rate the adjectives on a five-point Likert scale (ranging from 1 to 5). The scores for feminine and masculine adjectives are separately totaled to indicate femininity and masculinity traits.

Androgyny scores are obtained by subtracting one from the other (e.g., Femininity - Masculinity or Masculinity - Femininity). Smaller discrepancies indicate greater androgynous traits.

As all respondents in the present study were female, feminine scores were expected to be higher than masculine scores. The sex role of respondents was determined by subtracting masculine scores from feminine scores. Positive scores indicate more femininity (less masculinity), while negative scores indicate less femininity (more masculinity). Lower scores suggest higher androgyny, and higher scores indicate less androgyny.

Reliability and Validity

The checklist serves as a reliable and valid measure of sex roles. Reliability coefficients were computed using the split-half method, resulting in values of 0.78 and 0.81. The total item coefficient of correlation for masculine adjectives ranged from 0.42 to 0.75, while for feminine adjectives, the range was 0.42 to 0.73.

III. Marital Adjustment Questionnaire

The Marital Adjustment Scale, developed by Kumar and Rohatgi (1987), is utilized in the present study. This standardized scale was developed based on Indian samples (see Appendix III).

Scoring

The questionnaire comprises 27 highly discriminating Yes/No items. Its purpose is to categorize individuals into different groups based on their marital adjustment. For scoring, a "Yes" answer is assigned a score of 1, except for items 4, 10, and 19, where reverse scoring applies. The sum of these values yields the marital adjustment score. A higher total score indicates better marital adjustment. The following percentile norms categorize marital adjustment into five categories:

23.87 - 22.82: Very good

21.67 - 20.82: Good

20.01 - 18.22: Average

17.16 - 16.64: Poor

15.41 - 13.22: Very poor

Reliability & Validity

The Marital Adjustment Scale demonstrates both reliability and validity. The split-half method yielded a reliability coefficient of 0.70. Face validity is fairly high, and content validity was adequately assured. Additionally, the questionnaire was validated against Singh's Marital Adjustment Inventory (Singh, 1972). The coefficient of correlation between the questionnaire and Singh's marital adjustment inventory for a group of 20 wives was found to be 0.71, with an index of reliability of 0.84.

IV. Personal Data Sheet

A personal data sheet was designed to collect relevant information about respondents, including their present age, level of education, number of children, length of marital life, length of service, income, occupation, and family structure. Instructions on how to respond to the inventories and questionnaires were also included. Please refer to the appendix for the personal data sheet.

Design

The present study aims to investigate the relationship between three variables: self-concept, sex-role, and marital adjustment among educated employed and unemployed women groups.

Additionally, we intend to explore the interactional effects of these variables. Specifically, we will examine the impact of status on self-concept, sex-role, and marital adjustment. We'll also analyze the effects of self-concept on status, sex-role, and marital adjustment, as well as the effects of sex-role and marital adjustment on status, self-concept, and each other.

To assess the magnitude of the variables (self-concept, sex-role, and marital adjustment) and their differences between the two groups, we will compute the mean and perform a t-test.

We will also study the relationships between self-concept and sex-role (SC X SR), self-concept and marital adjustment (SC X MA), and sex-role and marital adjustment (SR X MA) in both groups using product moment correlation.

Furthermore, we plan to evaluate the effects of status, sex-role, and marital adjustment on self-concept. Specifically:

* The effect of status, self-concept, and marital adjustment on sex-role.

* The effect of status, self-concept, and sex-role on marital adjustment.

* The effect of self-concept, sex-role, and marital adjustment on status.

To analyze these effects, we will use a complex analysis of variance with a 2 X 2 X 2 factorial design.

Precautions

During data collection for this field study, we took several precautions:

* Respondents were approached individually and personally.

* In the employed women group, we avoided contacting more than two persons in one organization on the same day to prevent leakage of questionnaire information and discussions.

* Respondents filled out the data sheets personally.

* The study's purpose was clearly explained to participants to alleviate any fear or curiosity.

* The sequence of tests was pre-arranged to check for fatigue, boredom, and discussions during responses (ABC, BCA, CAB, BAC, ACB, and CBA order).

* To control response biases, respondents were assured that their answers would remain strictly confidential.

In some cases, only a few questionnaires were distributed in a specific area (for both employed and unemployed groups) to avoid mutual correspondence. Subsequent questionnaires were distributed only after receiving the filled-up forms from the initial batch of respondents.

Problems in Data Collection

The investigator encountered several challenges during the data collection process:

* **Not Interested:** Many respondents displayed little interest in participating and were unwilling to provide information, especially regarding their age, income, and qualifications. Some even declined to participate, citing lack of time or other commitments.

* **Non-Respondents:** A significant number of subjects did not return the questionnaires. In the present study, 20% of contacted participants failed to respond.

* **Incorrect Information:** Some subjects provided false information about their age, number of children, income, etc. Such data had to be either omitted or verified through records or repeated inquiries.

* **Reluctance in FillingMarital Adjustment Questionnaires:** Despite assurances of confidentiality, some respondents were hesitant to fill out the marital adjustment questionnaire. However, a few agreed to participate after receiving assurance.

Methodological Problems

In behavioral research, methodological issues arise in two main areas:

1. Research Methods: Researchers adopt specific approaches to study social phenomena. These approaches include:

* **Laboratory Research:** Controlled experiments conducted in a laboratory setting.

* **Field Experiment:** Research conducted in real-world settings, manipulating variables to observe their effects.

* **Field Study:** Observational research aimed at understanding interactions among sociological, psychological, and educational variables within natural social structures.

* **Survey Research:** Gathering data through questionnaires or interviews.

Measuring Instruments: The tools used to measure variables play a crucial role. For the study of self-concept, sex roles, and marital adjustment, researchers often employ correlational studies. Unlike experimental studies, which demonstrate functional relationships, correlational studies lack reversibility and exhibit symmetrical relations.

The Correlational Study and Measurement Instruments

The correlational study allows us to infer the presence or absence of a relationship between variables. However, it does not definitively establish the direction of the relationship. Therefore, a correlational study does not reasonably justify labeling one variable as independent and the other as dependent. Any statement about a causal connection between variables would be equally unwarranted.

Measuring Instruments

In psychological variable measurement, it is common to use causes and consequences of attitudes to measure the attitudes themselves. While this practice is accepted, it has an inherent weakness. A cause surrogate may also be a cause of attitudes other than the one under consideration. Similarly, an "outcome" surrogate may result from other attitudes as well. If such surrogates are used to measure the attitude of interest, it is essential to ensure that these "causes" and "consequences" are indeed related to the attitude being measured.

Some researchers suggest that careful item writing can mitigate potential biases. Others propose including items or scales that assess whether subjects are responding in a particular direction or in socially desirable ways. These safeguards aim to achieve an acceptable level of reliability and validity in measuring various constructs within the social sciences. Ultimately, this relates to the fundamental rationale of measurement theory.

Freeman (1950) emphasizes that self-report is the only available technique for measuring psychological variables such as self-concept, sex role, and marital adjustment. Rejecting self-report methods would significantly limit psychology's ability to explain behavior accurately. Therefore, psychology must approach these limitations with care and use the available information judiciously when assessing complex individuals.

Other Considerations

In the field of women's studies, several challenges arise. Ideological factors play a central role and are closely tied to the basic concepts of measurement. Additionally, technical factors related to the nature of the instruments used for data collection come into play.

Many statistical categories are underpinned by ideological assumptions, and this bias is deeply ingrained in widely used social science concepts. To address this, it is crucial to understand the origins of this bias and reconstruct these concepts to accurately represent the role of women in society. Furthermore, there is a pressing need for reliable data on the status of women in society.

In the present research, great care was taken to control and avoid methodological problems, ensuring objectivity in the findings.

CHAPTER III Effective Testing: Art of Inquiry

Self Concept, Sex Role, and Marital Adjustment Among Employed and Unemployed Educated Women

The present study aims to explore self-concept, sex role, and marital adjustment among employed and unemployed educated women. Data were collected from women in the urban area of Dhanbad. The employed group consisted of teachers from middle and high schools, college lecturers, professors, scientists, office staff from research institutes, government officers, and self-employed professionals.

The unemployed group included housewives whose husbands worked in similar occupations and organizations. All women in both groups were educated and matched based on age range, level of education, length of marital life, residence, family structure, and number of children, as far as practicable.

Given the increasing educational levels and changing status of women, several psychological variables are likely to change in response to their evolving conditions and environment. The study aims to investigate the extent, magnitude, and interactional effects of key psychological variables among educated employed women (study group) and compare them with educated unemployed women (comparison group).

The total sample size for this study is 400, with 200 employed and 200 unemployed women. The study focuses on the following independent variables:

Self Concept
Sex Role
Marital Adjustment

These three variables are correlated and have significant effects on each other. Additionally, status (employed vs. unemployed) is considered an important independent variable.

The main objectives of the study are as follows:

To determine the magnitude and direction of the variables under study.

To explore the relationship between self-concept (SC), sex role (SR), and marital adjustment (MA).

To examine the reciprocal interactional effects of these variables.

To assess the impact of employment status (E & UE) on self-concept, sex role, and marital adjustment.

Measurement tools used in the study:

Self Concept: Rastogi's (1979) "Self Concept Scale"

Sex Role Type: Sinha's (1986) "Masculinity-Femininity Check List"

Marital Adjustment: Kumar and Rohatagi's (1987) scale

The analysis of results is divided into three sections:

[Section 1]

[Section 2]

[Section 3]

Section - I

Section - I deals with the three psychological variables: self-concept, sex role, and marital adjustment. It examines their magnitude and the significant differences between these variables among both employed (E) and unemployed (UE) women groups.

Section - II

Section II focuses on correlations. It explores the relationships between:

* Self-concept and sex role

* Self-concept and marital adjustment

* Sex role and marital adjustment within the employed and unemployed women groups.

Section - III

Section III involves the Analysis of Variance. This part of the analysis investigates:

* The effect of one variable on another (interchangeably)

* Interactional effects among the three psychological variables (SC, SR, and MA)

* The impact of employment status on the above three psychological variables.

After collecting raw scores, the data were tabulated in a master chart and analyzed using relevant statistical techniques. The results are presented in tabular form in this chapter, along with graphical representations.

Section - 1

This section delves into the magnitude and direction of the three psychological variables: SC, SR, and MA. It is further divided into three sub-sections:

Section - IA

This sub-section provides results related to the magnitude of self-concept and its components. Additionally, it explains the significant differences in self-concept between educated employed and unemployed women groups.

Scoring of Self-Concept

As explained in the SC scale manual, higher scores indicate a stronger self-concept. For females, a score of 173 is considered an average self-concept score. Scores at or above 173 are categorized as higher self-concept, while scores below 173 indicate lower self-concept.

The results reveal the self-concept scores of employed and unemployed women groups, as well as the differences in self-concept scores between the two groups.

Employed Women Group:

Mean Self-Concept Score: 174.83

Interpretation: The employed women group has a higher self-concept score than the overall mean score provided in the manual.

Unemployed Women Group:

Mean Self-Concept Score: 171.05

Interpretation: The self-concept score of the unemployed women group is lower than the average mean score of the scale.

The above results indicate that the unemployed women group not only possesses a lower self-concept than the employed women group but also falls below the mean value of the scale. Conversely, the employed women group has a higher self-concept than the unemployed women group and surpasses the mean value of the scale.

Furthermore, the difference in self-concept between the two groups is statistically significant at the < .01 level. This supports Hypothesis No. 1: "Self-concept of employed women will differ significantly from that of unemployed women," rejecting the null hypothesis.

Perceptual Component:

Employed Women Group:

Mean: 25.42

Standard Deviation (SD): 3.29

Unemployed Women Group:

Mean: 22.79

SD: 3.31

The mean perceptual component score is higher among employed women than among unemployed women. Both groups score better on health and sex appropriateness items (perceptual components) than the mean value given in the scale, but there is a significant difference between the two groups (t-test value: 8.22, p < .01).

Conceptual Component:

Employed Women Group:

Mean: 66.36

SD: 10.03

Unemployed Women Group:

Mean: 64.62

SD: 8.36

The conceptual component of self-concept is lower in the unemployed women group compared to the employed women group. The mean difference is statistically significant (t-test value: 1.82, p < .01), supporting the partial hypothesis that "the conceptual component of self-concept will differ significantly among employed and unemployed women groups." The result rejects the null hypothesis. The mean value of the conceptual component for women (as given in the scale) is 52, and both groups exceed this value.

Unemployed Women Group Analysis

When the mean difference was tested using a t-test, the value obtained was 1.58, which is significant at the < .01 level. This result indicates that the unemployed women group significantly differs from the employed women group in terms of the attitudinal component of self-concept. Thus, it supports the partial hypothesis (Hypothesis 2) that "the attitudinal component of self-concept will differ significantly between employed and unemployed women."

The mean value of the attitudinal component of self-concept given in the manual is 102. However, the obtained mean for both groups is lower than the scale's mean value. This suggests that both groups possess a lower level of attitudinal self-concept than the average value indicated by the scale.

Components of Self-Concept:

Physical Component (PC) and Cognitive Component (CC): Both groups scored higher in PC and CC compared to the scale's mean value. This implies that women in both groups have a positive self-concept related to physical appearance, attractiveness, and sex-appropriateness (PC) as well as psychological aspects such as abilities, social adjustment, and personality traits (CC).

Affective Component (AC): Both groups scored lower in AC compared to the scale's mean value. This indicates that women, whether employed or unemployed, lack confidence in their present status, future prospects, self-worth, and feelings of pride and shame.

To gain a clearer understanding of self-concept magnitude among the two groups (employed and unemployed), we identified a high self-concept group based on scores equal to or higher than the mean value (173) in the scale. The following table displays the scores for the high self-concept groups of employed and unemployed women:

Table

Group N (High Self-Concept) Mean (M) Standard Deviation (SD)

Employed Women 108 196.32 9.32

Unemployed Women 84 184.35 8.95

The 't' value between the means (9.07) indicates a significant difference between the two groups. Thus, it supports the partial hypothesis (Hypothesis 3) that high self-concept scorers are more prevalent in the employed women group than in the unemployed women group, rejecting the null hypothesis.

Low Self-Concept Group Analysis

The low self-concept group comprises individuals who scored below the mean value (173) on the self-concept scale.

* Employed Women Group: 92 participants

Mean (M) of low self-concept scorers: 160.95

Standard Deviation (SD): 7.16

* Unemployed Women Group: 116 participants

Mean (M) of low self-concept scorers: 161.91

Standard Deviation (SD): 8.77

The t-value between the two means is 1.10, which is not significant. Therefore, there is no significant difference in low self-concept scores between the employed and unemployed women groups.

When considering the mean range of high and low self-concept for the employed women group (196.32 - 160.95) and the unemployed women group (184.35 - 161.91), it is evident that the employed women group has a higher range. Figure 3.6 illustrates the scores of the low self-concept group for both employed and unemployed women.

Sex Role Types (Section IB)

To assess sex roles, we used the Masculinity Femininity checklist developed by Sinha (1986). The checklist consists of 40 adjectives categorized as follows:

* Positive Masculinity (PM)

* Positive Femininity (PF)

* Negative Masculinity (NM)

* Negative Femininity (NF)

For calculating sex role scores:

* Masculinity scores were subtracted from femininity scores.

* This yielded androgyny scores (Feminine Masculine = Androgyny, denoted as FMA).

* Positive FMA indicates femininity (+F), negative FMA indicates masculinity (-M), and zero represents absolute androgyny.

Results:

Employed Women Group:

* Mean sex role score: 1.50 (SD: 8.51)

* The positive M score suggests more femininity.

* The M score is close to absolute androgyny.

Unemployed Women Group:

* Mean sex role score: 4.00 (SD: 6.96)

* The positive M score indicates femininity.

* The M score is higher than that of the employed women group, suggesting greater femininity and less androgyny.

* The 't' value between the means is 3.25 (significant at < .01 level).

Conclusion:

* The groups significantly differ based on masculinity and femininity traits.

* Hypothesis 4 is supported: "There will be a significant difference in sex role type scores between employed and unemployed women groups."

Sex Role Types Analysis

The results indicate the following counts for each sex role type within the employed and unemployed women groups:

Feminine Women:
Employed Women Group: 69
Unemployed Women Group: 79
Masculine Women:
Employed Women Group: 33
Unemployed Women Group: 32
Androgynous Women:
Employed Women Group: 98
Unemployed Women Group: 89
We categorized women based on their sex role scores:
* Absolute Androgyny (0 to 2): Women falling within this range.
* Feminine Type (+2 or more): Women with positive sex role scores.
* Masculine Type (below -2): Women with negative sex role scores.
Observations:
* There is no significant difference in the number of masculine-type women between the employed (33) and unemployed (32) groups.
* However, there is some difference in the number of feminine-type and androgynous-type women between the two groups.
Hypotheses:
Hypothesis 5 (Partial): There will be more androgynous/sex role type women in the employed women group than in the unemployed women group.

Hypothesis 5 (Rejected): There will be more masculine sex-role type women in the employed women group than in the unemployed women group.

To test for significant differences between the means of different sex role types in both groups, an 'I' test was computed.
Results:
* Mean (M) of feminine sex role type in the employed women group: 10.10 (SD: 3.74)
* Mean (M) of feminine sex role type in the unemployed women group: 11.99 (SD: 3.16)
* Sample size (N): Employed (69), Unemployed (79)
The 'I' test yielded a value of 1.38, which is not significant. Therefore, both groups are not significantly different from each other regarding feminine sex role type. Although the number of feminine-type women varies, the overall result suggests no significant difference.
Conclusion:

* While there is no significant difference in feminine sex role type, considering the number of women in both groups reveals some variation.

* Hypothesis 6 (Partially Supported): There will be a significant difference in the type of sex role (Feminine) between employed and unemployed women groups.

Masculine Sex Role Type:

The table above displays the scores for the masculine sex role type in both women groups. In the employed women group, there are 33 individuals with a masculine sex role type. The mean score for this group is (-9.06), with a standard deviation (SD) of 9.02. In the unemployed women group, the mean score for the masculine sex role type is (-10.50), with an SD of 5.59. A 't' test was conducted to determine if there is a significant difference between the means. The result yielded a value of 0.54, which is not statistically significant. Therefore, both groups do not significantly differ in terms of masculine sex role type. Consequently, the second part of hypothesis no. 6, which posits a significant difference in the type of sex role (masculine) between employed and unemployed women, is rejected, and the null hypothesis is sustained.

Androgynous Sex Role Type:

The data also reveals that there are 98 androgynous sex role type women in the employed group and 89 in the unemployed group. The mean score for androgyny in the employed women group is zero (0), with an SD of 3.21. In contrast, the mean score for androgyny in the unemployed women group is (-1.48), with an SD of 3.33. The 't' ratio between the two means is 3.15, which is statistically significant at the < .01 level. This indicates that both groups significantly differ in terms of androgynous sex role type. Thus, the results support hypothesis No. 6, which posits a significant difference in the type of sex role (androgyny) between employed and unemployed women, rejecting the null hypothesis in this regard.

Based on the persuasion of the M of sex role type, it is evident that the employed women group has fewer feminine and masculine sex role type women than the unemployed women group. Additionally, the employed women group has more androgynous sex role type women than the unemployed women group. Conversely, the unemployed women group either has more feminine or more masculine sex role type women than the employed women group, but fewer androgynous sex role type women.

Section - IC: Marital Adjustment

This section delves into marital adjustment, its magnitude, and the varying degrees of marital adjustment in both groups of educated employed and unemployed women. It also outlines the levels of marital adjustment.

Scoring of Marital Adjustment:

As per the manual of marital adjustment, higher scores indicate better marital adjustment. The scale provides the following norms for marital adjustment (M.A.):

23.87 - 22.81: Very Good Marital Adjustment

21.67 - 20.82: Good Marital Adjustment

20.81 - 18.47: Average Marital Adjustment

17.27 - 16.78: Poor Marital Adjustment

15.43 - 13.89: Very Poor Marital Adjustment

The data indicates a significant difference in marital adjustment scores between the employed and unemployed women groups.

The result shows that the obtained Mean and SD of the employed women group are 21.31 and 2.84, respectively. The Mean and SD of the unemployed women group are 21.19 and 2.65, respectively. Both groups' means fall within the "good" marital adjustment category. When the mean difference of marital adjustment was tested through a 't' test, the value was 21, which is not significant. This reveals that employed and unemployed women groups do not differ significantly in terms of marital adjustment. Thus, hypothesis no. 7, which states that "Marital adjustment of employed and unemployed women groups will significantly differ," is rejected, and the null hypothesis is sustained.

Figure 3.9 shows the Marital adjustment scores of employed and unemployed women groups.

The next result shows the number of women falling under varying degrees of marital adjustment in the employed and unemployed women groups. In the employed women group, there are:

* 80 women falling under the "very good" category

* 58 women falling under the "good" category

* 33 women falling under the "average" category

* 13 women falling under the "poor" category

* 16 women having a "very poor" marital adjustment

Similarly, among the unemployed women group:

*62 women fall in the "very good" category

*75 women fall in the "good" category

*36 women fall in the "average" category

***14 women fall in the "poor" category**

***13 women fall in the "very poor" category of marital adjustment**

In the "very good" category, there are more employed women (80) than unemployed women (62). However, in the "good" category of marital adjustment, the unemployed women (75) outnumber the employed women (58). Figure 3.10 illustrates the composition of employed and unemployed women groups based on varying degrees of adjustment.

For finding out the exact number of women with better marital adjustment or poor marital adjustment, high and low marital adjustment groups were computed based on Marital adjustment scores. A score of 22 and above is considered high MA, while below 22 is taken as low MA. The percentage of high/low M.A. groups in the employed and unemployed women groups was also calculated.

The results show that:

* In the employed women group, there are 174 women with high marital adjustment and 26 women with low marital adjustment.

* In the unemployed women group, there are 166 women with high marital adjustment and 34 women with low marital adjustment.

Among the employed women group, 87% have high marital adjustment, while 13% have low marital adjustment. In the unemployed women group, 83% have high MA, and 17% have low marital adjustment.

Section - II

Section II explores the correlations between self-concept & sex role, self-concept and marital adjustment, and sex role & marital adjustment in employed and unemployed women groups. The product-moment correlation between the variables was calculated to determine the magnitude and direction of the relationships. Three Product Moment ('r') correlations were computed to ascertain the relationship between the variables. The obtained "+" value is 3.13.

Co-efficient of Correlation between Self-Concept and Sex Role of Employed and Unemployed Women Groups

It was hypothesized that self-concept and sex role would be related in both employed and unemployed women groups. The table below shows that the correlation between self-concept (SC) and sex role (SR) in the employed women group is 62, which is significant at the < .01 level. This significant correlation indicates that both psychological variables are significantly correlated. Similarly, the correlation between SC and SR in the unemployed women group is 72, which has also yielded a significant result.

Thus, both psychological variables are significantly related in the context of unemployed women. Consequently, hypothesis no. 8, which states that "self-concept will be related to sex role type score in both employed and unemployed women groups," receives empirical support and retains the hypothesis, while the null hypothesis is rejected. The correlation between self-concept and sex role in both employed and unemployed women groups is positive in nature. This significant positive correlation suggests that women with high self-concept will possess a high sex role (i.e., feminine sex role, denoted as +F), whereas women with low self-concept will exhibit a low sex role (i.e., masculine sex role, denoted as -M). Therefore, the results indicate that higher self-concept is associated with greater femininity, while lower self-concept is linked to less femininity or more masculinity. Another correlation was computed to explore the relationship between self-concept and marital adjustment, separately for employed and unemployed women groups.

The 'r' value between the two for the employed women group is 39, which is significant at the < .01 level. This demonstrates that self-concept and marital adjustment are significantly correlated in the employed women group. The correlation is positive in nature, indicating that the level of marital adjustment increases with the level of self-concept, and vice versa. In other words, high self-concept is related to high marital adjustment (H.M.A.), while low self-concept is associated with low marital adjustment (M.A.) in both employed and unemployed women groups. The correlation between self-concept and marital adjustment in the unemployed women group is 0.16, which is also significant at the < .01 level. This finding further confirms that both variables are significantly correlated in the unemployed women group. Again, the direction of correlation is positive, suggesting that higher self-concept corresponds to greater marital adjustment, while lower self-concept is associated with lower marital adjustment in unemployed women. Thus, hypothesis no. 9, which posits that "self-concept will be related to marital adjustment in both employed and unemployed women groups," receives empirical support from the present results, and the hypothesis is sustained, while the null hypothesis is rejected.

Correlation was also computed to investigate the relationship between sex role and marital adjustment. The correlation was computed separately for the employed and unemployed women groups.

Correlation Between Sex Role and Marital Adjustment of Employed and Unemployed Women Groups

The correlation between sex role (SR) and marital adjustment (MA) for the employed women group is 0.48, which is significant at the < .01 level. This indicates that sex role and marital adjustment are significantly correlated among employed women. The positive correlation suggests that higher marital adjustment is associated with a more feminine sex role, whereas lower marital adjustment is related to a more masculine sex role in this group.

For the unemployed women group, the correlation between sex role and marital adjustment is 0.52, also significant at the < .01 level. This demonstrates that both variables are significantly correlated in the unemployed women group. Again, the positive direction of the correlation indicates that higher femininity (sex role) corresponds to higher marital adjustment, while lower masculinity (sex role) is associated with lower marital adjustment.

Therefore, the empirical results support Hypothesis No. 10: "Sex role type and marital adjustment will be related in both employed and unemployed women groups." The null hypothesis is rejected.

Section III: Analysis of Variance (ANOVA)

ANOVA is a parametric statistical method used to verify significant differences between means and explore interdependencies among variables. In this study, a complex $2 \times 2 \times 2$ factorial design ANOVA was applied to examine the effects of self-concept (SC), sex role (SR), and marital adjustment (MA) with status (employed and unemployed) as the independent variable. Three separate ANOVAs were computed to assess the main and interactional effects.

The first ANOVA investigates whether the degree of status, SR, and MA has any effect on SC separately and jointly. The hypothesis being tested is that there will be a significant interactional relationship between SC, SR, and MA among both employed and unemployed women groups. The present analysis aims to provide deeper insights into the relationship between these psychological variables for the two groups of women.

To calculate ANOVA, the scores for SC, SR, and MA were grouped into high and low categories. For SC, scores above the median (173) were considered high self-concept, while scores below were considered low self-concept. Similarly, HSR (high sex role) and LSR (low sex role) groups were determined based on SR scores. For marital adjustment, scores above the median (22) were considered high marital adjustment (HMA), and scores below were considered low marital adjustment (LMA).

Self-Concept (SC) Scores Among Employed and Unemployed Women

It was observed that the average SC scores for employed women were 173.13, while for unemployed women, the average SC score was 169.56. The difference between these scores was tested using an F-test, resulting in a significant finding at the 0.01 level. This significant F-ratio indicates that employment status has a notable impact on self-concept. In other words, the level of self-concept is influenced by whether a woman is employed or unemployed. This result aligns with previous research, where a t-test also demonstrated a significant difference between SC scores for employed and unemployed women. Thus, we can confidently support Hypothesis No. 1: "Self-concept of employed women differs significantly from that of unemployed women."

Impact of Sex-Role (SR) on Self-Concept (SC)

We further investigated the effect of sex-role (SR) on self-concept. SC scores were categorized into two levels: High SR (expressing femininity) and Low SR (expressing masculinity). The average SC scores for the High SR group (feminine females) in both the employed and unemployed groups were 173.2. For the Low SR group (masculine females), the average SC score was 169.48. However, when tested using an F-test, the result was 0.07, which is not statistically significant. Therefore, having a high degree of SR (femininity) does not necessarily lead to higher SC than having a low level of SR (masculinity). In other words, SC is not significantly affected by different types of SR.

Interestingly, a previous study found a positive and significant correlation between SC and SR for both groups. Specifically, SC increased with High SR (femininity) and decreased with Low SR (masculinity). However, ANOVA results did not fully support these findings. While the correlation between SC and SR remains positive, ANOVA provides a more accurate assessment of the impact of SR types on SC levels.

While computing ANOVA, the data were divided into finer levels. Specifically, eight cells of data were taken, with SC scores measured based on High Sex Role (HSR) for both employed and unemployed women groups. The result revealed a non-significant F ratio. This finding suggests that the level of self-concept (SC) is not significantly affected by the types of sex roles (SR). Consequently, the second part of hypothesis number 11, which posits that "women of masculine/androgynous sex role type will have high self-concept, whereas feminine women will have low self-concept," is rejected. However, the null hypothesis in this context—that "women of masculine/androgynous SR type will not necessarily have high self-concept, whereas feminine women will not necessarily have low self-concept"—is sustained.

The third aspect of ANOVA aimed to study whether the degree of marital adjustment (MA) among women has any effect on SC. SC scores were taken with respect to high and low MA groups. The average SC scores for the high and low MA groups were 171.81 and 170.87, respectively. When the F test was conducted, the resulting score was 0.62, which is also not significant. This non-significant result indicates that women with high MA will not necessarily have a high level of SC.

In contrast, the previous result showed a significant positive correlation between SC and MA for both groups. In other words, the level of SC increases with high MA (HMA) and decreases with low MA (LMA). However, this finding does not support the present result. As a result, the second part of hypothesis number 12—"women having good marital adjustment will have higher self-concept than women having poor marital adjustment" (partial)—is rejected based on the obtained result. The null hypothesis in this context—that "women having good marital adjustment will not necessarily have higher self-concept than women having poor marital adjustment"—is sustained.

Furthermore, ANOVA provided additional insights by examining finer relationships and their directions. The analysis revealed that the level of SC is not solely determined by the level of marital adjustment (MA), leading to the partial rejection of hypothesis number 12.

In the present analysis of variance, we also identified three first-order interactions among three variables and one second-order interaction among all three variables. The first-order interactional effect explores the impact of status and sex role (A × B) on SC. Notably, the joint effect of status and sex role on SC yielded a significant F ratio of 828.76. This result indicates that the SC of the HSR group (feminine females) in the employed women group significantly differs from the LSR group (masculine females) in the unemployed women group. In other words, the average SC scores of women with HSR (femininity) in both employed and unemployed groups and those with LSR (masculinity) in both groups significantly differ in their self-concept. Thus, hypothesis number 14 is sustained and supported by this finding.

Interestingly, while the previous result suggested that SR alone does not significantly affect SC, the current result demonstrates that when SR interacts with status (St), it does impact SC. Specifically, SC is affected by women's SR only when SR itself is influenced by employment status. In other words, status affects SR, which in turn affects SC.

To Investigate the Impact of Status and Marital Adjustment (MA) on Self-Concept (SC)

Status and Marital Adjustment Interaction:

* An F-test was conducted to explore the joint effect of MA and status (employed and unemployed) on SC. The result was significant, indicating that both factors influence SC. This supports Hypothesis 15. Specifically, the level of SC differs significantly based on employment status and MA.

Self-Role (SR) and Marital Adjustment Interaction:

The interaction between high and low MA and high/low SR was also tested. The significant result suggests that SC varies among different groups:

* High MA women with high SR (Feminine Female)
* Low MA women with low SR (Masculinity)
* High MA women with low SR
* Low MA women with high SR

Thus, SR and MA jointly impact SC, supporting Hypothesis 20.

Three-Way Interaction: SR, MA, and Status:

* We examined the effect of SR, MA, and status on SC. Using an F-test, we found a significant interaction (3441.5 ratio, Table 3.17, AXBX C, row G, $p < .01$). This suggests that the three factors are interrelated and jointly influence SC. Women with varying levels of SR, MA, and employment status significantly differ in their self-concept. Hypothesis 23 is supported, and the null hypothesis is rejected.

Effect of SC, MA, and Status on SR:

Another ANOVA was performed to assess the impact of SC, MA, and status on SR. We considered SR scores for eight groups (e.g., HSC & HMA, HSC & LMA, LSC & HMA, LSC & LMA) among employed and unemployed women. High SR scores represented femininity, while low SR scores represented masculinity. The average SR scores for both groups were analyzed.

Impact of Status and Marital Adjustment on Self-Concept (SC) and Sex Role (SR)

1. Status and SR Interaction:

The average SR scores for employed women are 6.42, while for unemployed women, they are 8.05. An F-test yielded a significant result (F ratio = 3.47), indicating that employment status affects SR. Specifically, the type of SR is influenced by whether a woman is employed or unemployed. This supports Hypothesis 4, which posits a significant difference in sex role types between these two groups.

2. Effect of Marital Adjustment (MA) on SR:

SR scores were categorized into high (HMA) and low (LMA) levels. The average SR score for HMA group is 7.17, and for LMA group, it is 7.29. The F-test result (F ratio = 1.73) is significant. Additionally, the positive correlation between SR and MA in both employed and unemployed groups supports the association between HSR (femininity) and HMA, as well as LSR (masculinity) and LMA. Thus, Hypothesis 13 (regarding marital adjustment and sex-role type) is supported.

3. SC and SR Relationship:

We investigated whether the degree of SC affects SR. The average SR scores for high and low SC groups are 6.83 and 7.64, respectively. However, the F-test result (F ratio = 1.02) is not significant. Therefore, the type of SR is not determined by SC levels. This finding contradicts Hypothesis 11, which proposed a link between high self-concept and masculine/androgynous sex-role type.

In summary, while employment status and marital adjustment significantly impact SR, SC does not directly determine sex-role type. The null hypothesis regarding women's self-concept and sex-role type is sustained by the present results.

Certainly! I've proofread and formatted your text while keeping the headings bold. Here's the revised version:

Impact of Status, Marital Adjustment, and Self-Concept on Sex Role (SR)

1. SC and SR Relationship:

In a previous ANOVA, when SC was considered as the dependent variable and the effect of SR as the independent variable, the result indicated that the level of SC does not depend on the level of SR. In the present ANOVA, when SC was considered as the independent variable and SR as the dependent variable, the result again showed that SR does not depend on SC. Therefore, it appears that neither SC determines SR nor SR determines SC. Both SC and SR are not determinantal to each other.

2. Status and Marital Adjustment Interaction:

The joint effect of status (employed and unemployed) and marital adjustment (MA) on SR yielded a significant F ratio. Specifically, SR differs significantly between highly maritally adjusted employed and unemployed women and their low-marital-adjustment counterparts. This supports Hypothesis 17, which posits that employed women with high marital adjustment will have masculine/androgynous sex-role types, while unemployed women with low marital adjustment will have feminine sex-role types.

3. Status and SC Interaction:

When examining the joint effect of status and SC on SR, the F ratio was 26, which is not significant. This implies that SR is not affected by the combination of status and SC. While the previous ANOVA showed a significant effect of status and SR on SC, the present result suggests that SR does not depend on status and SC jointly. Women with high or low SC in both employed and unemployed groups do not necessarily differ in their sex-role types. Thus, Hypothesis 16 is rejected.

4. MA and SC Interaction:

The F ratio for the interaction between high/low MA and high/low SC (Table 3.20, BX C, 6th row) was found to be significant. This indicates that significant differences in SR depend on the levels of MA and SC. In other words, women with different combinations of HMA/LMA and HSC/LSC will significantly differ in their sex-role types. This result supports Hypothesis 21 and rejects the null hypothesis.

Analysis of Variance (ANOVA) Results

1. Effect of SC on SR:

* In the previous ANOVA, when SC was considered as the dependent variable and the effect of SR as the independent variable, the result indicated that the level of SC does not depend upon the level of SR.

* In the present ANOVA, when SC was considered as the independent variable and SR as the dependent variable, the result again showed that SR does not depend upon SC. Thus, it appears that neither SC determines SR nor SR determines SC. Both SC and SR are not determinantal to each other.

2. Interaction Effects:

* We observe three first-order interactions between three variables and one second-order interaction among the variables.

* Status (Employed/Unemployed) and Marital Adjustment (MA) on SR:

* The joint effect of Status and MA on SR yielded a significant F ratio. This indicates that SR of highly maritally adjusted employed and unemployed women significantly differs from the SR of low-level maritally adjusted women in both groups.

* Hypothesis No. 17 is sustained: "Employed women with high Marital Adjustment will have a Masculine/Androgynous Sex Role type, whereas unemployed women with low Marital Adjustment will have a feminine Sex Role type."

Status (Employed/Unemployed) and SC on SR:

* The F ratio for the joint effect of Status and SC on SR is 26, which is not significant. Therefore, status (employed and unemployed) and SC do not jointly affect SR.

* While the effect of status and SR on SC was significant in the previous ANOVA, the present ANOVA shows that SR does not depend on the status and level of SC.

* Women with high or low SC in either employed or unemployed groups will not necessarily differ in their Sex-role type (Hypothesis No. 16 is rejected).

MA and SC on SR:

* The interaction between high/low MA and high/low SC (Table 3.20, BX C, 6th row) yields a significant F ratio. This implies that significant differences in SR depend on the level of MA and SC.

* Specifically, women with high MA and high SC, high MA and low SC, low MA and high SC, and low MA and low SC will significantly differ in their SR.

* The result supports Hypothesis No. 21 and rejects the null hypothesis.

Interaction of Self-Concept (SC), Marital Adjustment (MA), and Status on Sex Role (SR)

The third interaction studied in this three-way analysis of variance is between SC, MA, and Status on SR. SC and MA were considered at two levels (high and low), and status was categorized as employed and unemployed women. The F test yielded a significant result with an F ratio of 3.41 at the 0.01 level. This significant interaction indicates that the three factors—SC, MA, and status—do not act independently. Instead, they jointly influence SR. Different types of SR among women will significantly differ due to varying levels of MA, SC, and status. Thus, hypothesis No. 23 is supported, and the null hypothesis is rejected.

Effect of Marital Adjustment (MA) on Other Variables

The third ANOVA aimed to explore the impact of MA on various other variables. In this analysis, MA served as the dependent variable, and the effects of Status (St.), Self-Concept (SC), and Sex Role (SR) on MA were observed.

*** Status and MA:**

* The average MA scores for employed women were 20.60, and for unemployed women, they were 20.9.

* The F test for this difference was not significant (F ratio = 0.02). Thus, MA is not affected by employment status (employed vs. unemployed).

* This result aligns with previous findings and rejects hypothesis No. 7, which posited that marital adjustment would significantly differ between employed and unemployed women.

Effect of SC on MA:

* MA scores were compared between high and low SC groups.

* The average MA score for the high SC group was 21.13, while for the low SC group, it was 20.46.

* The F test yielded a significant result (F ratio = 6.52), indicating that women with a higher degree of SC exhibit better MA than those with lower SC levels.

* This finding supports the first part of hypothesis No. 12: "Women with a high level of self-concept will have better marital adjustment than women with a low level of self-concept."

In summary, the present results provide evidence for the relationships between SC, MA, and SR, while also shedding light on the impact of SC on MA. The null hypothesis is rejected in favor of these significant associations.

Next Aspect of ANOVA: The Impact of Sex Role (SR) on Marital Adjustment (MA)

In this section, we explore whether the type of SR has any effect on MA. We divided SR into two groups: high (Feminine) and low (Masculine), based on MA scores. The average MA scores for the high and low SR groups are 20.58 and 20.74, respectively. When we conducted an F-test, the resulting F-score was 1.81 (Table 3.23, 3rd row, column C), which is statistically significant. This finding indicates that MA is influenced by the SR type among both employed and unemployed women. In other words, women with high SR (Feminine) differ in their MA compared to women with low SR (Masculine). This result supports the first part of hypothesis no. 13 and rejects the null hypothesis in this context.

Interaction Effects: Status (SC) and SR on MA

We also examined three first-order interactions and one second-order interaction among the variables. The first interactional effect focuses on the joint impact of status (employed and unemployed) and SC on MA. However, the joint effect of status and SC on MA did not yield a significant F-ratio. This implies that MA is not significantly affected by the interaction between status and SC (high or low). Consequently, employed women with high SC, unemployed women with high SC, employed women with low SC, and unemployed women with low SC may not necessarily differ in terms of marital adjustment. Thus, we reject hypothesis no. 18 and uphold the null hypothesis that "Employed women with high SC will not necessarily have higher MA than unemployed women with low SC."

Joint Effect of Status and SR on MA

The F-ratio for the joint effect of status and SR on MA is 292.05, which is statistically significant. This result indicates that both status and SR jointly influence the MA of employed and unemployed women. Specifically, the level of MA depends significantly on the interaction between status and SR. In other words, women in the employed and unemployed groups with high SR (Femininity) and low SR (Masculinity) will differ in terms of their marital adjustment. Thus, hypothesis no. 19 is supported by the obtained result, and the null hypothesis is rejected in this context.

Effect of SC and SR on MA

We also tested the interaction between high/low SC and SR. The resulting F-ratio is 24.02, which is statistically significant. This finding suggests that there are differences in MA among women with high/low SC and high/low SR in both employed and unemployed groups. Specifically, the MA of women depends on their SC levels and SR types. Employed and unemployed women with high SC and high SR, high SC and low SR, low SC and high SR, and low SC and low SR will significantly differ in their marital adjustment. This result supports hypothesis no. 22 and rejects the null hypothesis.

The Interaction Between SC, SR, and Status on MA

In this three-way analysis of variance, we explore the interaction between SC, SR, and status (employed and unemployed) on MA. We categorized SC and SR into high/low levels. When we tested this interaction using an F-test, the resulting F-ratio was 313.68, which is highly significant. This finding indicates that all three factors (St, SC, and SR) are interrelated and jointly influence MA. Consequently, women at various levels will significantly differ from each other. Thus, hypothesis no. 23 is supported by the present result, and the null hypothesis is rejected in this context.

Concluding Remarks

* Based on the statistical results of the present study, we can safely conclude the following:

* Employed and unemployed women significantly differ in their SC and SR.

* However, they do not significantly differ in terms of their MA.

* SC and SR have a significantly positive correlation with each other and with MA.

* ANOVA results show that SC depends on the status of women, but the level of MA does not.

* Neither SC depends on SR nor SR depends on SC, but MA depends on SR, and SR also depends on MA.

* The level of MA also depends on the level of SC, and vice versa.

* The interaction between SR and status, MA and status, and MA and SR influences the level of SC.

* The interaction between MA and status, SC and MA influences the type of SR.

* However, SC interacting with status does not influence SR.

* Similarly, SR interacting with status influences MA, but SC interacting with status does not determine the level of MA.

* Finally, the level of SC, type of SR, and level of MA depend on the interaction among SC, SR, MA, and status.

CHAPTER IV Discussion: Unmasking Hidden Dynamics

Education, Employment, and Their Impact on Women's Personality

The recent changes in Indian society related to education and employment have significantly influenced the personality of women. In this context, the present study aims to explore self-concept, sex-role, and marital adjustment among educated employed and unemployed women, as these factors play a crucial role in shaping their overall personality.

The data for this study were collected from an urban population. Two groups of women were randomly selected. To ensure a representative sample, specific criteria were applied during the selection process:

* Respondents had to be educated at least up to the graduation level.

* They were married.

* Belonged to various types of organizations and mixed occupation groups.

* Had a minimum of four years of marital life.

* Fell within the age range of 25 to 50 years.

* Had varying numbers of children.

* Had a minimum of four years of tenure in their occupation.

Following these restrictions, two groups of women were identified:

1. Educated Employed Women: Considered as the study group.

2. Educated Unemployed Women: Considered as the comparison group.

Self-Concept and Its Components

Self-concept refers to an individual's perception of themselves, shaped by various structural components. It holds central and inclusive significance for each person, influencing all aspects of behavior, whether simple or complex (Hurlock, 1974). Hurlock identified three major components of self-concept:

Perceptual

Conceptual

Attitudinal

To measure self-concept and its components, we used the self-concept scale developed by Rastogi (1979), which aligns with Hurlock's framework.

Understanding Sex Roles

The term "sex-role" pertains to behaviors considered masculine or feminine within our culture. While people are often categorized as either masculine or feminine based on their interests, attitudes, and behaviors, the reality is more nuanced. Most individuals possess a combination of both masculine and feminine characteristics, making them androgynous (Bem, 1974, 1981, 1985; Helmreich, Spence, and Wilhelm, 1981; Spence and Helmreich, 1978).

Bem (1975) viewed masculinity and femininity as opposite poles along a single dimension. Consequently, the less masculine a person is, the more feminine they are perceived to be. Bem introduced the concept of psychological androgyny, where individuals exhibit both masculine and feminine qualities. To assess sex-role type (masculinity-femininity traits), we utilized a checklist developed by Sinha (1986), based on Bem's sex-role identity concepts (1975).

Marital Adjustment: An Overview

Marital adjustment can be defined as the mutual adaptation between husband and wife, leading to companionship, agreement on basic values, affectional intimacy, accommodation, euphoria, and other unidentified factors (Locke and Williamson, 1958). In broader terms, marital adjustment refers to the overall state of the marital relationship, where both spouses experience happiness and satisfaction with their marriage and with each other. The Marital Adjustment Questionnaire developed by Kumar and Robtagi (1987) measures the level of marital adjustment across various intensities.

The study's findings have been presented in quantitative, qualitative, and graphical terms in Chapter III. In the discussion section, we organize the results into three sections for analysis:

Section I: Self-Concept (SC), Sex-Role (SR), and Marital Adjustment (MA) variables.

Section II: Correlation between the variables.

Section III: Interaction effects and the impact of one variable on the others.

Section I: Self-Concept (SC)

The present investigation aims to compare self-concept (SC) between educated employed and unemployed women. The mean SC scores (Table 3.1) for employed women are 174.83, while for unemployed women, they are 171.05. The calculated 't' value between the two means is 4.14, which is significant at the 0.01 level. This result indicates that SC among employed women is significantly higher than that among unemployed women. According to the SC scale's manual, the median SC score is 172. Additionally, the employed women group surpasses the median value, whereas the unemployed women fall below it. These findings support Hypothesis No. 1, which posits that SC of employed women will differ significantly from that of unemployed women.

Self-Concept Components and Employment: A Comparative Analysis

Similar results were observed across the components of self-concept (SC). Specifically, in the perceptual, conceptual, and attitudinal aspects of self-concept, the employed women group scored higher than the unemployed women group. Both groups significantly differ concerning their SC components.

To further explore the higher and lower levels of SC within both employed and unemployed women groups, we computed additional data. The results revealed that the higher SC group of employed women significantly outperformed the higher SC group of unemployed women. This finding indicates that the high self-concept (HSC) level among employed women is notably better than that of the HSC group among unemployed women. Conversely, when comparing the lower SC (LSC) groups of employed and unemployed women, no significant difference emerged. In other words, the lower level of SC is relatively similar between both groups. However, the range of HSC is significantly broader among employed women.

The present study also aims to determine how employment contributes to enhancing SC. Based on the above results, it is evident that employment plays a crucial role in elevating the level of SC. Several related factors associated with employment contribute to the development of high SC.

Empirical studies support these findings. For instance:

* Gainor Kathy and Forrest Linda (1991) found that career positively influences SC.

* Jenkins, Sharom, Ral (1994) emphasized the impact of women's occupational roles, affiliative values, and power satisfaction on SC.

* Lenham Janel and Simonson (1990) reported significantly higher self-esteem among professional women compared to non-professional women.

The improved SC among employed women may stem from feelings of self-identity, self-respect, confidence, better socioeconomic status (SES), and positive feedback from others. Lenham, Janel, and Simonson (1990) highlighted the critical relationship between an individual's sense of identity (or self-identity) and self-esteem. Employment fosters confidence and a stronger sense of identity, ultimately enhancing SC.

Self-Concept, Employment, and Socio-Economic Status Among Women

Employment provides women with economic independence and contributes to their socio-economic status (SES). The economic status and independence also influence women's self-concept (SC). Hong Sung Morke (1982) found a significant relationship between socio-economic status and SC, which was consistent with results from Rao (1978), Drummond, Robert, and Melee Walter (1980), and Bledose, Joseph (1981). These studies hypothesized that economic status is the best predictor of SC and provided supportive evidence.

Economic independence and status also lead to positive feedback from others and social support for employed women. These factors play a crucial role in the development of high self-concept (HSC) among women, as SC is influenced by how others perceive oneself. Crosby, Richard (1982) supported this notion, emphasizing that a healthy self-concept is based on positive self-perception and recognition from others.

Furthermore, various studies highlight the contribution of social support to HSC. Muhlenkamp, Ann, and Sayed Judy (1986) found a positive association between self-esteem and social support. Raimy (1948) concluded that an individual's beliefs about themselves affect how others perceive them socially. Fey (1954) also discovered that self-acceptance is associated with being accepted by others. Factors such as self-perception, positive self-perception, social support, and social comprehension likely contribute to employed women's feelings of worthiness, self-importance, and prestige in society.

In the current social scenario, employed women receive social support and assistance from their spouses and children in household work. These factors may be responsible for the higher self-concept observed in employed women. Additionally, a woman's career plays a vital role in developing positive personality traits. Striving for equal privileges with men enhances confidence, self-respect, and self-concept. The present study also reveals a significant difference in the self-concept of educated career women, emphasizing that education and career contribute not only to earning but also to various psychological aspects valuable for women and society as a whole.

Sex Role

Sex role typing is the process by which children acquire the values, motives, and behaviors viewed as appropriate for either males or females in a specific culture. Traditionally, males are expected to be independent, assertive, dominant, and competitive in social relations. Females, on the other hand, are expected to be more passive, loving, sensitive, and supportive, especially in their family role as wives. However, the changing social scenario and the career-orientedness of women have started affecting the traditional sex roles. Women now feel entitled to many of the considerations and opportunities that were previously allowed to men alone.

This change has indeed impacted women's traditional sex roles. The present study aims to investigate the extent of sex roles among women today, considering the influence of employment and education. We compare employed women with educated non-working women.

To measure sex roles, we use the Masculinity-Femininity checklist developed by Sinha (1986). This checklist contains 40 adjectives related to two polarities of sex roles: masculinity and femininity (20 for each). Masculinity and femininity represent two opposite poles along a single dimension. As a personality construct, masculinity and femininity account for individual variations and indicators of adaptation. According to Mussen (1961), masculinity/femininity plays a role in overall adjustment.

Psychological androgyny is defined as a function of masculinity and femininity scores. Bem (1974) suggests that both masculine and feminine characteristics can coexist in the same individual. Those who exhibit a relatively high degree of both masculine and feminine traits are labeled as "androgynous."

In this theoretical context, masculinity and femininity are global, unidimensional concepts that refer to constellations of converging attributes and behaviors that normatively distinguish between men and women.

The results related to sex roles among employed and unemployed women show that both groups possess more feminine traits than masculine traits. The obtained scores for sex roles are positive (+) in nature. The mean score for employed women is closer to absolute androgyny (i.e., =O) compared to the unemployed women group. This indicates that employed women are less feminine than unemployed women but are also closer to absolute androgyny. The 't' value between the two means is significant, revealing that the groups differ significantly based on sex roles.

Self-Concept, Sex-Role, and Marital Adjustment Among Employed and Unemployed Educated Married Women

The results indicate that the number of androgynous women in the employed women group is higher than in the unemployed group. The number of masculine and feminine females is roughly similar in both groups, supporting each other's results. The difference in androgynous self-concept (SR) type between employed and unemployed women is significant.

The concept of androgyny was developed by Bem (1974) and further explored by Spence and Helmirich (1975). Bem argues that androgynous individuals fare better than purely masculine or feminine individuals because they can adapt appropriately to various situations. Bem's findings suggest that feminine females are less capable, with little difference between masculine and androgynous females. These findings align with the present study, where more employed women exhibit androgynous traits compared to unemployed women. It appears that employed women effectively balance both masculine and feminine qualities, allowing them to assert their rights and fulfill their duties both within the family (as females) and outside the home (in their professional roles).

While it is expected that all females would score higher in feminine traits, employed women also perform duties outside the home. Consequently, they are expected to exhibit higher levels of both masculine and feminine traits, making them more androgynous than unemployed women. Interestingly, the present study reveals that employed women still retain their feminine qualities even while performing masculine duties. Their feminine traits have not diminished due to employment, nor has their masculinity overshadowed their femininity. This balance qualifies them as androgynous.

Unemployed educated women, not being in the workforce, also possess more feminine traits than masculine ones. Despite societal changes and additional responsibilities (such as teaching their own children and managing external household affairs), their SR type remains consistent. In contrast, employed women exhibit visible changes in their SR type. The status of employment (employed vs. unemployed) significantly influences the SR type of educated women. Educated and employed women handle multifaceted tasks beyond the home, impacting their self-concept. Unemployed educated women, while performing domestic chores and other family-related duties, maintain their femininity. Unemployment seems to preserve their feminine qualities.

However, employment strongly affects the SR of employed women. They are more androgynous due to the additional responsibilities associated with their jobs. Balancing normal duties with employment obligations has led to the development of masculine traits alongside femininity. As an adjustment, employed women combine both traits equally.

Various studies also support the present finding. Bem (1974) explored that androgynous people are those who endorse both masculine and feminine traits, judged to be significantly more desirable. Here again, the above notion supports the findings that employed women who play both roles at home as well as outside the home are more appropriate to the prevailing situation and thus are more desirable. According to Locksley and Calten (1979), individuals high in both masculinity and femininity (in these global senses) are better adjusted than sex-typed individuals both psychologically and sociologically.

Spence et al. (1975) found that androgynous individuals have higher self-concept (SC) than do masculine, feminine, or undifferentiated subjects. Here again, it may be ascertained that employed women, due to employment, have higher SC as found in the present study, and due to this, they possess androgynous traits or vice versa. Many studies support an association between individual sex role (SR) orientations and women's aspirations (Lipman-Blumen, 1972). Employment also determines SR orientations. Smith I.D. (1975) analyzed the reciprocal effects of current SR attitude and employment.

Evidence from panel studies also indicates that the causal relationship between non-familial experience and sex role orientation is conditional either on the stage of the life cycle or age cohort (group). Employment and family responsibility constrain women's lives, but it also enhances confidence and helps in developing positive qualities because they can successfully solve problems in a routine way. To some extent, it also influences SR. That is why more androgynous women are found in the employed women group.

Hoffman (1977) studied the effects of rising maternal employment. She reported that "husbands of employed women help more in household tasks, including child care, than the husbands of unemployed women." This fact implies a convergence of SR in both males and females due to employment, as the present result also confirms the above findings.

The Impact of Employment on Marital Adjustment Among Indian Women

The present study aims to explore whether employment has any effect on the marital adjustment (MA) of Indian women. The study observed that the mean MA scores for employed and unemployed women groups were 21.31 and 21.19, respectively. The calculated "t" value between the means was 21, which was not statistically significant. This suggests that there is no significant difference in MA between employed and unemployed women. Interestingly, the overall MA in the unemployed women group was 4% higher than that in the employed women group.

Various studies have reported different results regarding MA in employed and unemployed women. Durkac and Judith (1987) found no significant relationship between housework division and marital satisfaction. This finding aligns with the present study, where no significant difference was observed in MA between employed and unemployed women.

Bem (1976) noted that androgynous individuals are better equipped to handle situational demands compared to strictly masculine or feminine individuals. In our study, we found a higher number of androgynous women in both employed and unemployed groups. This suggests that the level of MA in both groups may be influenced by the self-role (androgyny) of women in general. However, Jones, Cheñovetz, and Hansson (1978) reported a different result, emphasizing that masculinity, rather than androgyny, predicts greater adjustment and flexibility for both sexes.

Role conflict among working women has been associated with lower MA. Heckman et al. (1977) discovered evidence of role conflicts that can negatively impact personal identity and professional performance. In a recent study on role conflict and adjustment, Acharya (1998) highlighted that many informants found it challenging to balance societal expectations and their dual roles. Husbands, family members, neighbors, colleagues, and superiors often lack psychological preparedness to accept working women.

Surprisingly, our study did not find evidence supporting the concept of role conflict as a determinant of MA. No significant difference in MA was observed between the homogenous groups of employed and unemployed women.

Role Conflict and Marital Adjustment Among Employed Women

Role conflict may significantly impact the marital adjustment (MA) of employed women. Partners often have different role expectations, and these roles are culturally defined. Traditionally, men are expected to manage external responsibilities, while women are primarily responsible for internal household matters. Despite the additional workload and responsibilities that come with a career, employed women seem to successfully navigate this situation while maintaining good marital adjustment.

The present study focuses exclusively on Indian women, and its findings align with Indian societal norms. In the Indian context, marital adjustment remains a crucial aspect of women's lives, regardless of their employment status. As Kapadia (1958) expressed, "Marriage is a social duty towards the family and the community." According to traditional Indian norms, a woman's good MA plays a more significant role in determining her social status than her employment status (whether employed or unemployed). Additionally, factors such as the husband's status and job contribute to overall status.

Nye (1963) compared the MA of employed and unemployed women and found no significant difference. Similarly, Lockes and Mackprang (1949) reported no significant difference in marital adjustment between the two groups. However, Chesser (1956) discovered a definite association between occupation and marital adjustment among women. Hoffman (1963) supported the idea that wives' employment could increase marital conflict.

Despite these varying findings, it can be concluded that employment does not significantly affect the marital life of women. Career-orientedness is not the primary objective for most women. Both spouses and other family members prioritize family life, and they respect and accept women's status (whether employed or unemployed). Consequently, employed women achieve good marital adjustment, similar to their unemployed counterparts.

To Investigate the Relationship Between Self-Concept (SC), Sex-Role (SR), and Marital Adjustment (MA) Among Employed and Unemployed Educated Married Women

In this study, we aimed to explore the relationship between self-concept, sex-role, and marital adjustment among educated married women. Specifically, we examined how these psychological variables impact women's lives and relationships. Our data collection focused on urban areas, and we analyzed the results to draw meaningful conclusions.

Results

We computed product moment correlations to determine the relationship between SC and SR, SC and MA, and SR and MA. The obtained results are summarized in Table 3.13. Notably, both employed and unemployed women showed significant positive correlations in all three cases:

SC and SR:

The level of self-concept (SC) was positively associated with sex-role (SR). Higher SR scores in our study indicate greater femininity, suggesting that higher SC is linked to femininity.

SC and MA:

We found that higher self-concept is associated with better marital adjustment (MA), and vice versa. Women with a positive self-concept tend to have more successful marital lives.

SR and MA:

Similarly, higher SR (femininity) was related to better marital adjustment. These findings support our study hypotheses.

Interpretation

In simpler terms, feminine women with a strong self-concept tend to be better adjusted in their marital lives, and vice versa. The reason behind this association lies in the fact that both SC and SR are influenced by cultural patterns, identification, and behavior. They are learned through societal norms and expectations. Marriage, as an institution, is also shaped by societal norms, and marital adjustment reflects adherence to these norms. Thus, the positive influence of SC and SR on each other is natural and expected.

SC and Influencing Factors

Our study also revealed that SC is highly influenced by occupation, power satisfaction, and affiliative values (as discussed in Chapter 1).

Feminine Traits and Career Women

In our culture, feminine traits are highly appreciated. Even among career women, these feminine traits are not rejected. While working women may need to adopt some masculine qualities to meet job requirements, they still retain their femininity. This combination of feminine and masculine traits appears to contribute to better adjustment in various situations.

Dual Roles and Support

Employed women who juggle dual roles have learned to adapt to different situations. Their spouses often provide support, which contributes to better marital adjustment and enhances their self-concept. Unemployed women, possessing feminine traits and maintaining good marital adjustment, do not score as high in self-concept as employed women. In summary, employment status influences self-concept, sex-role type (androgyny), and marital adjustment in a reciprocal manner.

In conclusion, self-concept, sex-role, and marital adjustment are positively correlated with each other.

Certainly! I've proofread and formatted your text while keeping the original content intact. Here's the revised version:

Various Studies and Findings Support It

Regarding status, Lonham, Janel, and Simonson (1990) found that self-esteem is significantly higher in professional women compared to homemakers and non-professional women. Reo Pateat and Mary Martin (1991) implemented a career awareness program for adolescent girls and observed positive self-concept (SC) and confidence among them. Gainor, Kathy, and Forrest Linda (1991) discovered that career choice positively influences self-concept and marital happiness.

Various studies also indicate that high self-concept (HSC) is associated with sex-role (S-R) type. For instance, Burns (1977) revealed that self-perceived females' SC is related to femininity traits such as tenderness, sensitivity, and dependence.

In many cases, women choose jobs associated with their self-concept. Putnam and Hansen (1972) found that female subjects tend to select feminine role-concept occupations consistent with their self-concept. Consequently, it can be concluded that role conflict theory does not significantly influence employed women when they choose jobs aligned with their role appropriateness. This alignment contributes to enhanced self-concept and marital satisfaction, resulting in better marital adjustment (MA). Mackinnon (1978) also reported a statistically significant effect of sex roles on the employment of married women. They noted that the impact of S-R orientations on work behavior depends on marital status. This finding supports the assumption that job-related factors positively affect marital adjustment. Additionally, Jenkins and Sharom Raf (1994) found that women in relational power jobs reported affiliative values and interpersonal power satisfaction, which positively influenced self-concept and marital adjustment.

In summary, there is a reciprocal and interactional relationship between self-concept (SC), sex-role (SR), and marital adjustment (MA).

Section III

The aim of this section is to explore whether the degree of SC, SR, and MA is affected by status separately and jointly. Additionally, we will discuss the joint and reciprocal interactions and the effect of one variable on the other. We applied ANOVA to ascertain the effect of one variable on the others, providing results related to the dependence of these variables on each other. Previously, the "t" test revealed significant differences between the two groups concerning different variables. Various hypotheses in this regard were confirmed through ANOVA.

When status was considered as an independent variable, its effect on SC, SR, and MA was observed. The results showed that status significantly affects SC and SR. This implies that the level of SC and the types of SR depend on employment status (i.e., employed vs. unemployed). However, the effect of status on MA was not significant, indicating that the level of MA does not depend on women's employment status. These findings align with previous "t" test results. When we examined the effects of status, SC, SR, and MA as independent variables (interchangeably) on various dependent variables (SC, SR, and MA), the results were influenced by SC and SR, regardless of status. Specifically, SR is affected by MA but not by SC. Conversely, SC is not affected by MA or SR.

Certainly! I've proofread and formatted your text while keeping the original content intact. Here's the revised version:

In Summary

It can be concluded that marital adjustment (MA) and sex-role (SR) both mutually influence each other. However, self-concept (SC) is not directly affected by MA. Instead, the level of MA depends on SC, and neither SC nor SR directly depends on each other.

Results from ANOVA related to first-order interactions between variables—specifically SC & SR, SR & SC, and SC & MA as independent variables—were observed to understand their joint effects on SC, SR, and MA as dependent variables. The results revealed the following:

Status (ST) × SR Interaction:

* Combined status and SR significantly affect SC (Table 3.17, row D).

* Combined status and SR significantly affect MA (Table 3.21, row E).

Status (ST) × MA Interaction:

* Combined status and MA significantly affect SC (Table 3.17, row F).

* Combined status and MA significantly affect SR (Table 3.19, row D).

SC & SR Interaction:

* MA depends on the interaction between SC and SR (Table 3.21, row F).

* SR depends on the interaction between SC and MA (Table 3.19, row F).

* SC also depends on the interaction between SR and MA (Table 3.16, row F).

The first-order interaction results indicate that the level of SC depends on SR alone. When status interacts with SR, it also affects the level of SC. Additionally, when MA interacts with status, it influences the level of SC. The interaction between SR and MA also affects SC.

In summary, the level of SC depends on both status and the interactions between SC and SR, as well as SC and MA. The reciprocal interactions among status, SR, and MA play a crucial role in determining the SC level for women in both employed and unemployed groups.

Similarly, the results show that the level of SR depends on status alone, as well as the interactions between status and MA (St & MA) and SC and MA (SC & MA). However, the level of SR does not depend on the interaction between status and SC (St & SC).

Likewise, the level of MA does not depend solely on status. Instead, it is influenced by the interactions between status and SR (St & SR) and SR and SC (SR & SC). Notably, the level of MA does not depend on the interaction between status and SC (St & SC).

Furthermore, second-order interactions (joint interactions) reveal that SC, SR, and MA, along with status, interact reciprocally, impacting each other positively. These findings are supported by significant F ratios in the ANOVA results (Table 3.17, 3.1, 3.19, and 3.21).

In Summary: The Relationship Between Self-Concept (SC), Sex-Role (SR), and Marital Adjustment (MA) in Educated Married Women

The study explores the impact of employment on marital adjustment in Indian women, focusing on cultural factors, family dynamics, and other variables affecting self-concept and marital adjustment. Based on the results, we can draw the following conclusions:

First-Order Interaction Effects:

* The interaction between SC and SR significantly affects SC (Table 3.17, row D).

* The combined effect of status (ST) and SR significantly affects MA (Table 3.21, row E).

* The combined effect of ST and MA significantly affects SC (Table 3.17, row F) and SR (Table 3.19, row D).

* However, the interaction between ST and SC does not affect SR (Table 3.19, row E) or MA (Table 3.21, row D).

* MA depends on the interaction between SC and SR (Table 3.21, row F), while SR depends on the interaction between SC and MA (Table 3.19, row F). SC also depends on the interaction between SR and MA (Table 3.16, row F).

Level of SC:

* SC depends on SR alone. When status interacts with SR, it affects the level of SC.

* The reciprocal relationship between status, SR, and MA plays a crucial role in determining the SC level for both groups of women.

Level of SR:

* SR depends on status alone and the interactions between status and MA (St & MA) and between SC and MA (SC & MA).

* However, SR does not depend on the interaction between status and SC (St & SC).

Level of MA:

* MA does not depend on status alone. Instead, it relies on the interactions between status and SR (St & SR) and between SR and SC (SR & SC).

* The level of MA does not depend on the interaction between status and SC (St & SC).

Second-Order Interaction:

* SC, SR, and MA, along with status, interact reciprocally, affecting each other.

* The ANOVA results (Table 3.17, 3.1, 3.19 & 3.21) confirm this positive reciprocal impact.

Many factors related to status contribute to the enhancement of self-concept (SC) in employed women. These factors include prestige, recognition, acceptance, and appreciation. Employed women have their needs met in these areas, leading to a better SC compared to unemployed women. This aligns with previous research findings, as discussed earlier.

Hurlock (1974) identified three major components of SC: Perceptual, Conceptual, and Attitudinal. Among these, the attitudinal component plays a crucial role in determining high SC in employed women. It encompasses attitudes about present status, future prospects, feelings of worthiness, and self-esteem.

As status influences feelings of efficiency and competence, employed women tend to receive more respect, appreciation, and acceptance. Their economic stability contributes to overall satisfaction. SC is a continuous, learned behavior, and individuals continuously discover new potentials within themselves. The sense of achievement observed in employed women positively influences their SC development, as supported by the present study and other findings.

Additionally, employed women often exhibit outgoing behavior and maintain an up-to-date and presentable appearance. These factors contribute to the perceptual component of SC. Similarly, conceptual aspects arise from feelings about abilities and disabilities. Employed women develop a sense of worthiness and social usefulness due to their jobs, further supporting the study's results.

Socioeconomic status (SES) also plays a crucial role in SC development, as evidenced by studies such as Hong Sung Mook's (1982). Other researchers, including Rao (1978), Drummond, Robert, Mclatire Walter (1980), and Blendose, Joseph (1981), have provided supportive evidence.

Occupation has its own impact on SC, reflected in the characteristics of employed women. Jenkins and Sharom-Ra (1994) found better self-concept, power satisfaction, and affiliative values among employed women. Similarly, Lenham, Janel, and Simonson (1990) reported significantly higher self-esteem in professional women compared to homemakers and non-professionals. These findings highlight the crucial relationship between an individual's sense of identity and self-esteem, particularly in women. Gainor, Kathy, and Forrest Linda (1991) also observed that career positively influences self-concept in American women.

The self-concept (SC) is a product of reflexive activity and refers to an individual's overall self-evaluation (Rosenberg, 1965). Various aspects of self-esteem have been differentiated, such as the sense of power and sense of worth (Gecas, 1971), evaluation and affection, and sense of competence and self-worth (Smith, 1975). Self-evaluation and self-worth are also interconnected (Brisselt, 1972).

In the present study, it is evident that self-role (S-R) is heavily influenced by societal norms (St). This influence can be explained through several factors. At birth, biological sex identity is determined. Subsequently, children learn sex-role behavior based on fixed societal norms. Gender roles have been converging and changing in recent years. Women now intend to pursue careers, and to balance work and household responsibilities, they exhibit androgynous traits (Lacksley & Calten, 1979).

Interestingly, the unemployed women in the study displayed more feminine traits than the employed women. Since SR is a learned behavior shaped by societal norms, this finding aligns with Indian cultural values that appreciate femininity as a positive aspect of women's personalities. Even as women enter the workforce, they retain their feminine qualities while also developing some masculine traits. Notably, these results do not support the findings of Berns et al. (1977), who suggested that SR identity remains unchanged (Burns, 1977; Broverman et al., 1972).

Both groups of women (employed and unemployed) in the study exhibited more femininity traits than masculinity traits. One possible reason for this lies in the influence of biological factors, such as hormones and brain development, on SR. Pertinent and pubertal periods are critical in terms of hormonal responses in organisms (Goy, 1975; Hines, 1982; Hoyenga & Hoyenga, 1979). While these biological factors play a role, culturally prescribed SR has a considerable impact on women's role responses. For instance, young mothers tend to be more responsive to babies than childless women (Nash, 1973).

Another factor contributing to the observed results is that employed women may choose feminine-type occupations due to sex-role typing. Consequently, their sex-role remains relatively unchanged. Putnam and Hansen (1972) found that female subjects often choose employment based on feminine role concepts. Various other factors related to femininity and status have been discussed earlier (Section I).

Results related to the effect of status (employed and unemployed) on marital adjustment (MA) (Table 3.21) reveal that a non-significant F ratio exists between the two. This implies that status does not significantly impact MA, and conversely, MA is not significantly affected by the joint interaction of status (employed and unemployed) and levels of self-concept (SC) (HL). However, the effect of SC and sex-role (SR) on MA is significant. Additionally, the first-order joint effect (St & SR, SC & SR, and St & SC) on MA is highly significant.

Based on these findings, we can safely conclude that employed and unemployed women significantly differ in their SC and SR, but they do not significantly differ in terms of their MA. Furthermore, the level of MA does not depend on their employment status. This result aligns with the focus of our study on Indian women and their association with Indian societal norms. In the Indian context, marital adjustment remains a crucial aspect of women's lives. As Kapadia (1958) expressed, "Marriage is a social duty towards the family and the community." Similarly, Locke and Williamson (1958) explained that marital adjustment involves companionship, agreement on basic values, affectional intimacy, accommodation, euphoria, and other unidentified factors.

Considering traditional Indian norms, a woman's good MA plays a more significant and effective role in determining her social status than her own employment status (whether employed or unemployed). Additionally, in Indian society, a woman's status is still largely influenced by her husband's status rather than her own.

The ANOVA results also indicate that SR is not dependent on SC, and vice versa. This means that women with high SC will not necessarily possess high SR, and vice versa. The reason behind this may lie in the learned behavior of SR, which is culturally influenced. Various sources contribute to the conception of SR, and it varies across different life stages. While theories of SC suggest that SR operates in the formation of SC, our study's results challenge this theoretical explanation. Here, SC and SR are not as interrelated as previously thought. Instead, what appears more critical is an individual's ability to manage the situation they face and their success in dealing with those circumstances. Contrary to traditional concepts, our findings reveal that femininity is also associated with high SC. In other words, feminine or masculine (SR) personality traits are less effective in determining women's SC compared to their successful roles.

In today's educated society, equal regard is typically given to both males and educated employed females. Feminine roles are also valued. Educated women retain their feminine qualities while possessing high SC. Thus, SC is not solely determined by SR, and vice versa. Instead, SC depends on the appropriateness of the situation, while SR adapts to the requirements of the circumstances.

The Relationship Between Self-Concept, Sex-Role, and Marital Adjustment Among Employed and Unemployed Educated Married Women

The obtained results indicate that highly self-concept (HSC) women tend to have greater marital adjustment (MA). Specifically, when examining the effect of self-concept (SC) on marital adjustment, the F ratio is highly significant. HSC women experience better MA due to factors such as acceptance, appreciation, worthiness, respect, recognition, efficiency, and prestige. These positive feelings contribute to their overall satisfaction.

Additionally, employed women have more opportunities to interact with others, which helps them better understand people and develop diplomatic skills. This enhanced social interaction contributes to better adjustment capabilities, including improved MA. In the context of marriage, which is considered a sacred bond between husband and wife, these factors play a positive role.

Jenkins and Rat (1994) explain that women in relational power jobs report affiliative values and interpersonal power satisfaction, leading to good SC and positively influencing MA. Gainor Kathy and Forrest Linda (1991) found that educated working women exhibit HSC, which correlates with better MA.

Nye (1963) discusses the SC of employed women. Employment itself is relatively satisfying for well-educated women in professional and high-status occupations. It enhances self-respect and fosters satisfying interpersonal relationships. This positive feeling associated with employment likely affects MA. Woods, Nancy, Lentz, Martha, and Mitchell, Ellen (1993) discovered that married women experiencing less stress are better educated, better adjusted, and have higher SC.

The study also examined the effect of MA on SC. Interestingly, a non-significant F ratio suggests that MA does not significantly impact SC. In other words, women with high MA do not necessarily exhibit high SC. This discrepancy may be because SC increases with status, while MA remains unaffected by status. Women prioritize adjustment, but today's women do not rely solely on marital satisfaction for their self-worth. Instead, SC increases with status, providing a sense of worthiness and self-appropriateness.

Indian women embody certain societal values, including sacrifice and love. Even after marriage, a woman's SC remains intact and unaffected by marital life. However, the findings suggest that modern women are not solely satisfied by being successful housewives or mothers. Working women, despite facing challenges, take pride in their work and possess HSC alongside marital adjustment. Factors such as income (better SES) and support from spouses and society contribute to this dual satisfaction.

Next Aspect: The Effect of Self-Concept (SC) on Marital Adjustment (MA)

A significant F ratio indicates that SC significantly affects MA. In this context, MA serves as the dependent variable, while SC acts as the independent variable. The situational nature of SC contributes to its impact. Nelson (1996) notes that girls' self-development relies on mutually empathic relationships with primary caregivers. Additionally, Simon and Simon (1975) found a significant relationship between self-esteem and standardized academic achievement for both sexes. Ziller (1973) highlights the role of child-rearing practices and family environment in shaping children's SC.

Marital Adjustment (MA) and Sex-Role (SR)

The present study reveals a significant F ratio between MA and SR. When examining the effect of MA on SR and vice versa, both show a significant relationship. Indian women often embody the ideal of being adaptable and homely housewives. Those who identify as ideal feminine women strive to adjust well within their families and marital lives. Similarly, Indian women seeking better MA adhere to societal norms or their husband's expectations to achieve positive marital outcomes.

In Indian families, specific conduct is expected from both spouses and other family members, based on fixed societal roles. Conformity with these prescribed behaviors is essential for achieving good MA. As Goode (1965) notes, marriages in some societies are arranged primarily for duty and mutual respect rather than personal happiness. Clear role specifications within larger society facilitate smoother interactions and greater agreement on duties and rights.

Traditional Marriage Roles and Harmony

Traditional marriage roles leave little room for conflict, as both husband and wife find satisfaction in fulfilling their expected roles (SR). Cormac (1961) emphasizes that the differentiation of sex and function, without competition, contributes to feminine power and women's fulfillment. The present study supports this notion, suggesting that possessing more feminine traits correlates with higher marital adjustment.

Even when women take on additional roles or responsibilities due to employment, they continue to act according to their prescribed roles as wives and mothers. Successfully balancing these roles is akin to a career in itself. Mirdal and Klein (1956) observe that women willingly accept the dual responsibilities of work and motherhood, seeking harmony within themselves.

In the Present Study: The Relationship Between Marital Adjustment (MA) and Sex-Role (SR)

A significant F ratio has been found between marital adjustment (MA) and sex-role (SR). The results indicate that when the effect of MA was tested on SR and vice versa, a significant F ratio was observed. This suggests that the marital adjustment of women is influenced by their sex-role, and conversely, their sex-role is affected by marital adjustment.

The ideal image of Indian women is that of an adaptable and homely housewife. Naturally, women who identify themselves as ideal feminine individuals strive to display these traits and adjust better within their family and marital life. Similarly, Indian women who seek better marital adjustment must adhere to society's fixed norms or meet their husband's expectations, as revealed in the present study.

In Indian families, specific behavior is expected from both husbands and wives, as well as from every family member, based on predefined societal roles. To achieve good marital adjustment, everyone is bound to act in accordance with these prescribed norms. As Goode (1965) notes, "In only some societies have marriages been arranged primarily for the personal happiness of the husband and wife." Instead, the focus is on fulfilling duties and showing mutual respect.

The traditional concept of marriage leaves no room for conflict, as both husband and wife find satisfaction in fulfilling their expected roles (SR). Cormac (1961) emphasizes that the differentiation of sex and function, without competition, is crucial for feminine power and the fulfillment of womenhood. The present study also supports this idea, showing that possessing more feminine traits is associated with higher marital adjustment.

To maintain harmony and happiness in married and family life, women continue to act according to their prescribed roles, even when faced with additional responsibilities from their jobs. Being a successful wife is a career in itself, and if a woman chooses another career, she must reconcile the two roles to achieve inner harmony. As observed by Mirdal and Klein (1956), "They have willingly accepted their dual responsibilities as workers and mothers; their challenge lies in harmonizing these roles." They achieve this by combining their home and work roles through socially prescribed femininity.

In summary, while the traditional view may suggest that a married woman's gainful employment outside the home is incompatible with being a good wife and mother, millions of married working women serve as living proof to the contrary.

Finally, based on the results obtained from the ANOVA, it can be explained that the entry of married women into the labor force leads to certain changes in their sex roles as influenced by their status. This interaction between status (S) and sex role (SR) has a positive effect on women. Additionally, it enhances the self-concept (SC) of employed women.

Employed women exhibit feminine traits, but they also lean toward androgynous traits, which appear more suitable for their situation. Women in dual roles—balancing responsibilities at home and in the workplace—demonstrate greater adaptability.

In traditional Indian contexts, women primarily focus on balancing their roles at home and in the workplace. Employment introduces a new dimension to their personality, as they take on additional responsibilities beyond their domestic duties. The interplay of status and sex role significantly impacts the self-concept of women. Similarly, when status combines with marital adjustment (MA), it positively influences their overall well-being and marital satisfaction.

Employed women with a stronger self-concept tend to be more content with their achievements. Their sex role traits align with the demands of their situation. Higher socio-economic status contributes to better self-concept. This, in turn, affects their sex role positively.

For employed women, exposure to a changed environment fosters adaptability and adjustment. This creates a harmonious family atmosphere based on love. Economically independent employed women are less demanding of their husbands, promoting cohesion within the family.

Status also plays a role in marital satisfaction. When combined with marital adjustment, it contributes to women's overall contentment. The resulting empowerment significantly boosts self-esteem. Professional women exhibit multifaceted personalities, and employment exposes them to diverse situations and people. Their adaptability contributes to better marital adjustment on the domestic front. Overall, these factors build women's confidence, enhancing both their self-concept and sex role.

Status, Self-Concept, and Marital Adjustment Among Employed and Unemployed Educated Women

1. Introduction: It may also be said that status does not affect self-concept (SC) among those women where there is no backup from the family and spouse. If the status has not been given due importance by the family, spouse, or society, and their status has not been appreciated, or they are not allowed to change their sex role (SR), the SC of women would not be affected by the status. In all these situations, conflict will act negatively, and it would not support enhancing the SC of women. The reason may be that SC is a situational learned process through culture and societal norms. Since the very beginning, the female child is subjected to a particular type of mental orientation based on reconciliation and compromise, rather than conflict, with regard to her married life. Even in cases where women are employed or holding status, they would not allow any rupture to embitter their married life. Thus, it may be said that SC will be affected by status only if SR and marital adjustment (MA) will also interact.

2. Self-Concept and Sex Role: The SR is not affected by the joint effect of status and SC. Possibly, women—whether employed or unemployed—want to retain their feminine attributes because these are considered very natural and normal for females. Nowadays, feminine traits are appreciated in women. They feel glorified by being feminine, and thus, they want to retain their femininity. Today's women are a harmonious blend of beauty (femininity) and brain. Employment affects the SC, SR, and MA of women. It has a positive effect on the overall personality makeup of women.

3. Reasons Behind Better Marital Adjustment in Employed Women: The reason behind better MA and retaining femininity traits in employed women may be due to the structure and culture of our society. Girls in Indian households grow up under a profound influence of their mothers, whom they have seen adjusting and making compromises in their marriages throughout their childhood and during their maturity, until they themselves get married and become wives. Thus, adjustment and compromise become a part of their nature. Moreover, our religion, tradition, culture, and society regard marriage as a very sacred bond, stronger than any other relationship. Once a girl gets married, the husband gains complete rights over her life, and he becomes her topmost priority, even more than her parents. However, society also views marriage as a holy relationship, and a troubled marriage is looked at with disrespect. This perspective strengthens the relationship. Additionally, women are generally highly religious, and they believe that "marriages are made in heaven." Psychology drives them, and anything beyond it just does not occur to them.

4. Conclusion: Despite the rapid strides made in various fields, our social mindset remains primarily puritanical. Feminism is expected and appreciated in women. Moreover, women are the ones who keep a traditional Indian home—a "home." This truth holds today as it did years ago. While status may bring fancy houses, if it results in a broken home, it will never be accepted. Instead, it will putrefy our society.

The Relationship Between Feministic Traits, Employment, and Self-Concept Among Women

Introduction: The results have shown that both working women and housewives exhibit feministic traits. However, the findings also indicate that working women tend to have a more androgynous nature—a balanced mix of both masculine and feminine traits—which is highly desirable. This observation aligns with various research studies.

The Influence of Employment on Feminine and Masculine Traits: The reason behind this phenomenon seems to be the blending of feminine traits typical of traditional Indian housewives with masculine traits due to exposure to employment. Working women retain their desirable feminine qualities while gradually adopting the toughness and resilience required in the professional world. Traditional Indian women often exhibit an abundance of feminine traits, including maternal instincts, caring nature, soft-spoken demeanor, and grace. However, the demands of the workplace encourage women to develop ruggedness and resilience. Consequently, exposure to employment contributes to an increase in the masculinity level of their personality, resulting in an androgynous profile.

Self-Concept and Its Components: It is essential to consider that employed women are expected to exhibit both masculinity and femininity traits, placing them closer to androgyny. The present study reveals that the self-concept of working women is higher than that of non-working women—an unsurprising result. As proposed by Harlock (1974), self-concept comprises perceptual, conceptual, and attitudinal components.

Perceptual Component: This aspect relates to how individuals perceive their outward appearance, including physical looks, body image, and appropriateness of their sex. Working women, often outgoing and concerned about presentation, take care of their appearance, potentially boosting their self-concept.

Conceptual Component: Feelings about abilities and disabilities contribute to self-concept. Employment provides a sense of worthiness and social usefulness, reinforcing faith in one's abilities and enhancing self-concept.

Attitudinal Components: Employed women may experience positive self-identity, self-respect, confidence, better socioeconomic status (SES), and positive feedback from others—all of which contribute to their overall self-concept.

Impact of Employment and Education: The present study aimed to explore the impact of employment on the psychological makeup (self-concept, sex role, and marital adjustment) of educated women. Positive results indicate that employment plays a significant role in the changing social landscape, benefiting betterment, upliftment, and adjustment. While employment and education positively affect self-concept and sex role, marital adjustment remains unaffected. In summary, both employed and unemployed women adapt to the dynamic demands of society while maintaining their family relationships, traditions, and values associated with family, children, and marriage. Their devotion remains steadfast.

CHAPTER FIVE

Conclusions: Key Findings

On the basis of the obtained results and considering the purpose of the study, the following conclusions may be drawn:

Self-Concept (SC):

* The self-concept of employed women is higher than that of unemployed women. Additionally, employed women's self-concept surpasses the mean value given in the SC scale.

* Unemployed women not only exhibit lower self-concept than employed women but also score below the mean value of the scale. This difference can be attributed to various career-related factors, including occupation, affiliation, self-identity, self-confidence development, positive feedback, economic independence, socioeconomic status (SES), and societal acceptance.

Components of Self-Concept:

* Self-concept comprises three major components: perceptual, conceptual, and attitudinal.

* Employed women score significantly higher than unemployed women in all three components.

* Specifically, employed women score higher in the perceptual (PC) and conceptual (CC) components compared to the mean value in the scale. However, they score lower in the attitudinal (AC) component.

* Unemployed women also score higher than the mean value in the perceptual and conceptual components but fall short in the attitudinal component. Despite this, employed women still outperform unemployed women in the attitudinal aspect. The need for further improvement remains.

Sex-Role (SR) Type:

* Both women groups exhibit more feminine traits than masculine traits.

* Employed women lean less toward femininity and are closer to absolute (-) androgyny than unemployed women. This difference can be attributed to the impact of employment status on SR.

* Interestingly, both groups have more androgynous females than strictly masculine females. Moreover, a higher proportion of employed women fall into the androgynous category compared to unemployed women.

* The changing societal scenario, dual roles (inside and outside the home), and appreciation of androgynous traits contribute to this phenomenon.

Marital Adjustment (MA):

* There is no significant difference in MA between the two groups.

* Regardless of employment status, Indian women prioritize maintaining good marital and family life. Employment remains a secondary objective, and societal norms and roles guide their behavior.

The Relationship Between Self-Concept (SC), Sex-Role (SR), and Marital Adjustment (MA) Among Educated Employed and Unemployed Married Women

1. SC and SR Correlation:

* The results indicate a positive correlation between self-concept (SC) and sex-role (SR). Specifically, women with high self-concept tend to exhibit more femininity than masculinity, while those with low self-concept show the opposite trend. This finding aligns with the societal emphasis on feminine traits in females, contributing to the enhancement of self-concept.

2. SC and MA Correlation:

* A significant positive correlation exists between SC and marital adjustment (MA) in both employed and unemployed women groups.

* Higher self-concept corresponds to better marital adjustment, and vice versa. In other words, women with a positive self-concept tend to have more satisfying marital lives.

* Several factors contribute to this relationship:

Opportunities for Interaction: Employment provides women with more opportunities to interact with others, understand problems, and develop effective coping strategies.

Empathy and Understanding: Employed women comprehend their husbands' job-related challenges, which enhances their own self-concept.

Problem-Solving Skills: The ability to solve problems easily and achieve satisfaction positively influences both self-concept and marital adjustment.

3. SR and MA Correlation:

* A significant, positive correlation exists between SR and MA.

* Higher marital adjustment corresponds to greater femininity (SR), while lower marital adjustment is associated with more masculinity.

* This finding reflects societal preferences for feminine traits in women.

4. Purpose of the Study:

* The study aims to explore the influence of one variable on another and the reciprocal relationships between SC, SR, and MA.

5. ANOVA Results:

Employment status significantly affects SC. The level of SC varies based on employment status (employed vs. unemployed).

The Relationship Between Self-Concept (SC), Sex-Role (SR), and Marital Adjustment (MA) Among Educated Employed and Unemployed Married Women: Additional Insights

SR and Employment Status:

* The results indicate that the type of sex-role (SR) is influenced by employment status (employed vs. unemployed).

* Specifically, more androgynous traits are observed among employed women compared to unemployed women. Additionally, employed women exhibit differences in SR type due to their employment status.

MA and Employment Status:

* Surprisingly, the level of marital adjustment (MA) is not significantly affected by employment status.

* Whether employed or unemployed, women with high marital adjustment (HMA) and those with low marital adjustment (LMA) do not significantly differ from each other. This finding underscores the importance of marital satisfaction regardless of employment status.

SR and SC Relationship:

* Contrary to expectations, the level of self-concept (SC) does not necessarily correlate with the degree of SR (femininity or masculinity).

* Different types of SR do not consistently impact the level of SC. The appropriateness of behavior in a given situation and the situational requirements play a crucial role in determining both SC and SR.

SC and SR Independence:

* The level of SC is not a direct determinant of SR type. Women with high SC may not necessarily exhibit high femininity (SR) compared to those with low SC.

* SR is a learned behavior influenced by cultural norms and various life experiences. Multiple factors contribute to both SC and SR.

MA and SC Relationship:

* The level of MA is influenced by the level of SC.

* Women with high self-concept experience acceptance, appreciation, respect, recognition, and flexibility. These positive feelings contribute to their overall satisfaction, affecting both SC and MA.

* In summary, SC significantly impacts MA, emphasizing the interconnectedness of these psycho-social variables.

The Relationship Between Self-Concept (SC), Sex-Role (SR), and Marital Adjustment (MA) Among Educated Employed and Unemployed Married Women: Further Insights

MA and SR Type:

* The results indicate that the level of marital adjustment (MA) is influenced by the sex-role (SR) type in both employed and unemployed women groups.

* Specifically, women with high SR (femininity) differ in their levels of MA compared to those with low SR (masculinity).

* This finding can be explained by considering the dual roles that women often play. A successful wife's role is akin to a career, and when a woman chooses another career (such as employment), she must reconcile these roles to achieve harmony within herself. Thus, SR positively impacts MA.

Type of SR and MA:

* The type of SR also affects the level of MA.

* Women identifying with high SR (femininity) and those adhering to low SR (masculinity) exhibit differences in their levels of marital adjustment.

* The ideal image of Indian feminine women involves being adaptable and homely. Naturally, women who perceive themselves as ideal feminine figures strive to display these traits and adjust better within their family and marital life, as evidenced by the present study.

Interaction Between Status (St) and SR on SC:

* The interaction between employment status (St) and SR significantly impacts self-concept (SC).

* Employed women with feminine SR, employed women with masculine SR, unemployed women with feminine SR, and unemployed women with masculine SR all differ in their SC levels.

* The dual role of employed women enhances their adaptability, allowing them to balance home and workplace demands. Additionally, status adds new dimensions to their personality, positively influencing SC.

Joint Effect of Status (St) and SR on MA:

* The joint effect of St and SR reveals that the level of MA varies based on both employment status and SR type.

* Employed women with feminine SR, employed women with masculine SR, unemployed women with feminine SR, and unemployed women with masculine SR all exhibit different levels of marital adjustment.

* Factors contributing to this variation include feelings of achievement, contentment, better socioeconomic status (SES), recognition from spouses and family members, and the impact of status (employment) and adjusted SR (based on situational requirements).

The Relationship Between Self-Concept (SC), Sex-Role (SR), and Marital Adjustment (MA) Among Educated Employed and Unemployed Married Women: Further Insights

Joint Interaction Between Status (St) and MA on SC:

The ANOVA results reveal that the level of self-concept (SC) significantly differs due to the joint interaction between employment status (St) and marital adjustment (MA).

Specifically, employed women with high marital adjustment (HMA), employed women with low marital adjustment (LMA), unemployed women with HMA, and unemployed women with LMA exhibit distinct levels of SC.

This finding can be attributed to the multifaceted nature of professional women. Adaptability, a hallmark of their dual roles, contributes to better marital adjustment on domestic fronts. As a cumulative effect, women gain confidence, enhancing their self-concept.

Joint Interaction Between St and MA on SR:

The results indicate that unemployed women with low marital adjustment (LMA), unemployed women with high marital adjustment (HMA), employed women with LMA, and employed women with HMA differ in their sex-role (SR) types.

This difference is explained by the feeling of self-satisfaction due to employment and the better marital adjustment abilities associated with more androgynous traits.

Joint Interaction Between St and SC on SR:

Interestingly, the joint interaction between employment status (St) and self-concept (SC) does not significantly impact SR types.

Employed women with high self-concept (HSC), employed women with low self-concept (LSC), unemployed women with HSC, and unemployed women with LSC do not differ significantly in their SR types.

This result aligns with the natural inclination toward feminine attributes in women today. Regardless of employment status, women strive to maintain a harmonious blend of beauty (femininity) and intelligence.

Joint Interaction Between SC and SR on MA:

A significant result emerges from the joint interaction between SC and MA.

Differences in marital adjustment (MA) occur among women with high self-concept (HSC) and high sex-role (SR) types, whether employed or unemployed.

In other words, MA depends on both the level of SC and the type of SR exhibited by women.

Joint Effect of SC and MA on SR:

The results also show a significant relationship between SC, MA, and SR.

The type of SR (masculine/feminine) depends on both the levels of MA and SC.

These psycho-social variables are intricately connected in shaping women's experiences and behaviors.

The Relationship Between Self-Concept (SC), Sex-Role (SR), and Marital Adjustment (MA) Among Educated Employed and Unemployed Married Women: Further Insights

Joint Effects of SR and MA on SC:

The results indicate a significant relationship between self-concept (SC) and the joint effects of sex-role (SR) and marital adjustment (MA). Specifically, the levels of SC (high or low) depend on the types of SR (masculine or feminine) and the levels of MA.

Second-Order Joint Interactions Between St, SR, and MA on SC:

Women with varying levels of SR, MA, and employment status (St) significantly differ in their SC. Status significantly influences SR, which can be explained by perceptual and conceptual components. The perceptual component relates to physical appearance, body image, and sex appropriateness, while the conceptual component arises from feelings about abilities and disabilities. Employed women, who pay attention to their appearance and have greater confidence in their abilities, exhibit higher SC.

Second-Order Joint Interactions Between St, SC, and MA on SR:

Status (St) also impacts SR significantly. Women with better SC tend to have better MA, and there is a reciprocal interaction between St, SC, and MA that affects SR. Societal norms and family expectations play a role, with femininity still being more appreciated than masculinity among Indian women.

Second-Order Joint Interactions Between St, SC, and SR on MA:

Women with varying levels of SC, SR, and St significantly differ in their marital adjustment (MA). The joint interaction of St, SC, and SR significantly affects MA. Better SC and androgynous sex roles lead to better adjustment in married life. In Indian society, adjustment and compromise are learned behaviors, contributing to the intricate relationship between these psycho-social variables.

CHAPTER SIX

Summary: In a Nutshell, Highlights of the study

The Changing Roles of Educated Women in India: Insights into Self-Concept, Sex Roles, and Marital Adjustment

In recent decades, Indian women have achieved a new status by adding the role of working professionals to their existing responsibilities. Research studies indicate that the attitudes of educated women, particularly those who work, have significantly evolved, especially concerning marriage, family, and social standing.

Education has transformed women's lives, equipping them with knowledge and skills. As educated women enter formal work settings, they break away from traditional social structures and networks.

Contemporary Indian women find themselves at the intersection of a traditional past and a modern future fueled by their dreams and aspirations. However, they often grapple with uncertainty about their self-worth and competencies.

This study focuses on the lives of educated married women, both employed and unemployed. It sheds light on the changing societal position of educated married women, emphasizing key psychological variables such as self-concept, sex roles, and marital adjustment.

Self-Concept:

Self-concept encompasses all aspects of an individual's being and experiences that are consciously perceived. Hurlock (1974) provides a more specific definition, describing self-concept as having three major components:

1. Perceptual Component (Physical Self): This relates to an individual's physical appearance and body image.

2. Conceptual Component (Psychological Self): It arises from feelings about one's abilities and disabilities.

3. Attitudinal Component (Attitudes): This component reflects an individual's attitudes toward themselves.

Changing Landscape Due to Education:

Education has rapidly transformed societal norms. Women are now more aware of their rights and have entered the workforce. While women in earlier decades were often associated with feminine qualities, the changing social landscape and career-oriented mindset have impacted traditional gender roles for Indian women.

Sex-Role Identity:

An individual's conceptualization of their degree of masculinity and femininity constitutes their sex-role identity. Some people exhibit predominantly masculine or feminine interests, attitudes, behaviors, preferences, and perceptions. However, most individuals possess a blend of both qualities, and some are androgynous. Bem (1981) suggests that androgynous individuals tend to be better adjusted because they can adapt appropriately to various situations.

Ideological Positions on Sex Roles:

Three main ideologies shape contemporary views on women's roles:

Conservative Ideology: This ideology emphasizes the lifelong pursuit of the "women's housewife role."

Moderate Ideology: It seeks a compromise between women's roles as mothers and working professionals.

Radical Ideology: Advocating absolute gender equality, it rejects moderate positions and supports the redistribution of work between men and women.

Marital Adjustment Among Educated Married Women: A Study on Self-Concept, Sex-Role, and Psychological Well-Being

Marital adjustment refers to the process by which a husband and wife adapt to each other, fostering companionship, shared values, emotional intimacy, accommodation, and other unidentified factors. According to Locke and Williamson (1958), marital adjustment encompasses characteristics such as conflict resolution, satisfaction with the marriage, common interests, and fulfillment of marital expectations.

In the traditional Indian context, marriage is considered a sacrament, uniting two individuals in an eternal and indissoluble union. Broadly speaking, marital adjustment reflects the overall happiness and satisfaction experienced by both partners in their marriage.

The present study investigates the relationship between self-concept, sex-role, and marital adjustment among employed and unemployed educated married women. As societal norms evolve, women have gained legal and political rights, education, and awareness of their rights, leading to shifts in attitudes. Work has acquired deeper meaning in women's lives, prompting many educated women to pursue various jobs. The investigator aims to understand the changes occurring among these working women concerning their self-concept, sex-role, and marital adjustment.

Self-concept plays a pivotal role in shaping human behavior. It influences motivation, direction, and the maintenance of psychosocial well-being. By examining self-concept among working and non-working women separately, the study seeks to analyze the impact of social comparison, feedback, and appraisal on their self-perception.

Sex-role differentiation has been widely studied, particularly in terms of coordinating work and family roles. Investigating the psychological masculinity and femininity of educated employed and unemployed married women sheds light on the coping strategies they employ to meet the demands of daily life.

Finally, the study explores how successfully educated married women manage harmony and happiness in their marital life. By assessing the extent of marital adjustment, the research aims to uncover the impact of added roles on the marital patterns of educated employed married women.

Marriage, Self-Concept, and Sex-Role: An Exploration of Marital Adjustment

Marriage holds immense significance in an individual's life. As societal norms evolve and women increasingly pursue career-oriented paths, traditional gender roles are being challenged. Women now aspire to opportunities that were previously reserved for men, leading to shifts in their roles. In light of these changes, the investigator seeks to understand the interplay between personality traits—specifically self-concept, sex-role, and marital adjustment.

The study aims to address several key questions:

1. Influence of Employment Status: How does employment status (employed vs. unemployed) impact the personality makeup of contemporary women? To explore this, the study focuses on three psychological variables: self-concept, sex-role, and marital adjustment. This exploratory investigation aligns with qualitative studies that shape the research agenda in the work-family-personality domain.

2. Components of Self-Concept: Self-concept comprises conceptual, perceptual, and attitudinal components. By analyzing these components separately among both study and comparison groups, the study aims to reveal micro-level differences in self-concept.

3. Changing Sex-Role Concepts: Investigating the various types of sex-roles within both groups sheds light on evolving sex-role concepts in the present context.

4. Marital Adjustment Strength: The study assesses the strength and magnitude of marital adjustment among employed and unemployed women, both individually and collectively. It seeks to understand how work impacts marital adjustment and how educated women navigate marital life.

5. Relationship Between Variables: The study explores the relationship between self-concept, sex-role, and marital adjustment. Understanding their interconnections is crucial.

6. Complementary Variables: Recognizing that psycho-social conditions influence variables, the study examines their complementary nature. By assessing magnitude and direction, it aims to uncover the impact of psycho-social factors.

7. Reciprocal Influence: Finally, the study investigates how one variable influences another, exploring reciprocal relationships.

Sample:

Study on Family-Work Domain and Personality Dynamics of Women

The present field study aims to test hypotheses related to the interplay between family, work, and personality dynamics among women. Two groups of women were randomly selected from the urban population of Dhanbad for this purpose:

Educated Employed Women: This group consists of women who are employed and have at least a graduate-level education.

Educated Unemployed Women: This group comprises women who are educated but currently unemployed.

All respondents in both groups are married. To ensure comparability, efforts were made to match the two groups in terms of age, education level, length of marital life, residence, family structure, number of children, and socioeconomic status (SES). The total number of respondents in the study is 400, with 200 in each group.

Measures Used:

Self-Concept Scale: The study employed Rastogi's (1979) self-concept scale. This standardized, self-administered scale assesses self-concept using positive and negative items distributed across three components.

Femininity-Masculinity Checklist: Developed by Sinha (1986), this standardized scale includes 20 feminine and 20 masculine items. It categorizes adjectives into four groups: Positive Masculinity (PM), Negative Masculinity (NM), Positive Femininity (PF), and Negative Femininity (NF).

Marital Adjustment Questionnaire: The study utilized a standardized questionnaire developed by Kumar and Rohtagi (1987). This questionnaire consists of highly discriminating "yes-no" type items related to marital adjustment.

Personal Data Sheet: A customized data sheet collected relevant information about the respondents.

CHAPTER SEVEN

Results: Data Reveals Emerging Trends

Results Analysis: Self-Concept, Sex Role, and Marital Adjustment Among Educated Women

The study results were analyzed in three sections:

Section I: This section examines the magnitude and direction of self-concept, sex role, and marital adjustment among educated employed and unemployed women. It also investigates significant differences between the two groups in terms of these variables.

Section II: Here, we explore correlations between the following pairs of variables:

* Self-concept and sex role

* Self-concept and marital adjustment

* Sex role and marital adjustment

* These analyses are conducted separately for both educated employed and unemployed women groups.

Section III: The third section focuses on joint and interactional effects of one variable on another.

Key Findings:

Self-Concept (SC):

* The self-concept scores of educated employed women significantly differed from those of unemployed women. Employed women scored better than the standard scale value, across all three components of self-concept.

* The employed women group exhibited a closer alignment with absolute androgyny, while unemployed women leaned more toward femininity.

Sex Role:

* Both groups displayed more feminine traits, but unemployed women exhibited a higher degree of femininity compared to employed women.

* The employed women group demonstrated a balanced mix of masculine and feminine traits.

Marital Adjustment (MA):

* There was no significant difference in marital adjustment between employed and unemployed women.

* High and low scorers in marital adjustment were similar across both groups, with a slightly higher percentage of highly adjusted women in the employed group.

These findings shed light on the complex interplay between self-concept, sex role, and marital adjustment among educated women, highlighting the nuances of their experiences in different life contexts.

Correlation Between Self-Concept, Sex Role, and Marital Adjustment Among Educated Women

The study revealed significant correlations between self-concept (SC), sex role (SR), and marital adjustment (MA) among both employed and unemployed women groups. Let's delve into the findings:

SC & SR Correlation:

* A positive and significant correlation exists between self-concept and sex role. Women with high self-concept tend to exhibit high femininity (SR), while those with low self-concept lean toward masculinity (LSR).

SC & MA Correlation:

* Higher self-concept corresponds to higher marital adjustment in both employed and unemployed women groups.

SR & MA Correlation:

* A positive and significant correlation links sex role to marital adjustment. Women with higher femininity (SR) tend to have better marital adjustment (MA), and vice versa.

Interpretation:

* Women with high self-concept and femininity traits experience better marital adjustment.

* Conversely, women with high marital adjustment and femininity traits also exhibit high self-concept.

* The employed and unemployed women groups differ in self-concept and sex role but not in marital adjustment.

Interaction Effects:

First-order interactions:

* Self-concept (SC) interacts with status (St) but does not affect sex role (SR) or marital adjustment (MA).

* Other first-order interactions (St & SR, St & MA, SC & SR, SC & MA, SR & MA) show significant results.

* St & SC on SR and St & SC on MA yield non-significant results.

Second-order interactions:

* All variables (St, SC, SR) interact significantly in relation to marital adjustment (MA).

Social Implications:

* Social changes are occurring due to women's dual roles (education and employment).

* Educated employed women exhibit better self-concept, contributing to their personal growth and future prospects.

* Parents' self-concept influences their children's development, emphasizing the importance of positive self-concept for future generations.

In summary, SC, SR, and MA reciprocally influence each other, with status playing a pivotal role. These findings underscore the evolving landscape shaped by women's multifaceted roles.

Results and Conclusions

The study revealed a trend of convergence in sex roles among employed women. Both groups of women were found to exhibit feminine traits, but the employed women group was closer to androgyny.

The impact of employment is evident in the changing social landscape, and this change has positive implications for betterment, upliftment, and adjustment. Employment and education positively influence self-concept (SC) and sex-role (SR), while marital adjustment (MA) remains unaffected. Based on the study findings, we can safely conclude that both employed and unemployed women adapt to the demands of our fast-changing and dynamic society while maintaining their family relationships and adhering to family values associated with marriage and children.

Limitations of the Study

1. Data Collection: The present study is a field study where collected data plays a crucial role. However, gathering data from over 400 women, while substantial, may have inherent limitations.

2. Methodology: Data for this research were obtained through questionnaires and checklists, which have their limitations in terms of discrepancies between behavioral and attitudinal measures expressed through the questionnaire.

3. Sample Selection: The sample consists of educated urban women. While this provides valuable insights, results may vary when considering different types of women or geographical areas.

4. Causality: The study does not explore causal factors related to low marital adjustment or self-concept. Additionally, respondents' responses were not compared to those of professionals who choose not to pursue dual careers.

5. Variable Focus: The study focuses on specific variables. Future research should consider additional important variables and their relationships.

6. Another Limitation of the Study, The researcher acknowledges a limitation in the study: the sample consisted entirely of urban women from Dhanbad. This raises concerns about the generalizability of the findings. In future research, it would be valuable to replicate these findings on a broader sample to yield more globally applicable results.

Practical Implications and Suggestions for Further Research

Here are the major practical implications:

1. Policy Formation for Women: Given the study's focus on family-work dynamics and women's personality, it highlights the need for careful policy formulation related to women. Policymakers should consider the unique challenges faced by women in balancing work and family responsibilities.

2. Assessing Welfare Reform Effects: If welfare reform becomes a reality, further research could assess its impact on women's working status. Understanding how policy changes affect women's employment can inform future reforms.

3. Dynamics of Dual-Career Women: To gain a more complete understanding of successful functioning among dual-career women, continued research in this area is essential. Investigating personality dynamics within couples can provide valuable insights.

5. Comprehensive Study on Self-Concept, Sex Role, and Marital Adjustment: A more accurate examination of self-concept, sex roles, and marital adjustment could involve studying both spouses. Collecting information from husbands can help counterbalance potential social taboos faced by married women when discussing their marital life. Assessing husband's psychology and cooperation levels would shed light on these variables.

Books By Dr Rekha Rani

Dr Rekha Rani's Thesis -

Topic - To study self-concept, sex-role and marital adjustment among educated, employed and unemployed women. (Vinoba Bhave University, Hazaribag, Jharkhand, India).

Study materials by Dr Rekha Rani'For NOU

Study material for for M. A. Psychology, Nalanda Open University written by Dr Rekha Rani -

1. Manovaigyanik Sanykhiki (Part of Khand Kha) - General Psychology

2. Sangyanatmak Manovigyan (section -A) - Statistics

3. Vyaktitv ka Manovigy (Section- B) - Personality

Hindi books by Dr Rekha Rani

1. Zindagii ke rang - Mari kuch kahaniyan

2. Zindagii ke rang - Mari kuch kavitayen

3. Galon par ek til- upnyas/novel

4. Chandni aur salman - story for children

5. Ishq aur Ibadat , what you truly love - English to Hindi translation of of rumi's poems

6. Vandana- magahi to Hindi translation of spiritual Magahi poems

7. Ruhaniyat - Kavita sangrah

8. Kuch Lafz Kuch Khyal - Kavita sangrah

9. Women in Workforce - Balancing Identity and Marital Bond (A complete research work by Dr Rekha Rani)

10. Krishna - Picture book story for children

Dr Rekha Rani's books are also available on

*** Notion Press** http://notionpress.com/author/300008

*** Kindle** linktr.ee/drrekharani

***Amazon** linktr.ee/drrekharani

*** Blog** - rekhasahay.com

*** Instagram** - rekhasahay8

*** YourQuote** - https://www.yourquote.in/drrekharani

*** Mail id** - rekhasahay8@gmail.com

dr_rekha_rani@yahoo.com